JOEL A. FREEMAN, PH.D. AND DON B. GRIFFIN

Return to Glory

◆ ◆ The ◆ ◆ ◆
Powerful
Stirring of the
Black Man

Return to Glory
The Powerful Stirring of the Black Man

by Joel A. Freeman and Don B. Griffin

Published by
RENAISSANCE PRODUCTIONS, INC.
537 Mantua Pike, Suite 203
Woodbury, NJ 08096

Library of Congress Catalogue Number: 96-072658
ISBN: 0-9625605-7-x

Unless otherwise indicated, Scripture quotations are from the New King James Version, © 1982 by Thomas Nelson, Inc., Nashville, Tennessee.

The Afterword, "The Admiral, David Robinson," is reprinted by permission of the American Tract Society.

This book contains stories of real people and real situations. Most people's actual names have been included, but some names have been fictionalized for protection and privacy.

Edited by Eugene Seals
Cover Art by Shango McDuffy
Design by Blum Graphic Design

Printed in the United States of America

Return to Glory

Essay Contest

It is our hope that this book and contest will serve as a catalyst for community pride, personal achievement and racial healing. The Essay Contest is designed to encourage an active participation by teenagers and young adults in recognizing their potential, assessing their circumstances and plotting their successful road to adulthood.

CONTEST RULES

1. The contest is open to all who have personally read *Return to Glory* and are 12 years or older, regardless of gender or race, except that no employees/relatives of Renaissance Productions, Joel Freeman or Don Griffin are eligible.

2. No entry fee is required for participation.

3. Write a two (2) page essay, without outside assistance, that reflects what you have received from the book, *Return to Glory,* entitled "How This Book Has Changed My Outlook on Life." It is to be printed or typewritten (single or double spaced) on regular 8-1/2" x 11" white paper. Send only one sheet with page one on the front and page two photocopied on the back. Name, mailing address, age and telephone number must be at the upper right hand corner of page one. The author's signature at the bottom of page two indicates that all of the information contained in the essay is true and that he/she is indeed the sole author of the work. Essays longer than two pages will be disqualified. One page essays are acceptable.

4. All essays become the property of Renaissance Production and may not be acknowledged or returned. Winners will be required to sign and deliver to Renaissance Productions a publicity release, permission to reprint and an affidavit of eligibility. Submitted essays may be used in future works by Joel Freeman, Don Griffin or Renaissance Productions.

5. Late, mutilated or previously published materials are not eligible and will not be considered. The contest manager's determination regarding late, mutilated, lost or previously published material shall be final. Renaissance Productions assumes no responsibility for entries.

6. The essays will be judged upon their consistency with the theme, honesty, creativity, use of real life illustrations and neatness as determined by the panel of judges. Essays must present a clear message of how the book has changed the contestant's outlook on life. Regional panels consisting of English and/or history professors/teachers from historically black colleges and universities and journalists from predominantly African American publications will judge the essays. All deci-

sions of the judges are final. First, Second and Third place winners will be selected in each of the seven regions. The following are the age categories: junior high school (12–15); high school (16–18); college (19–23) and adult (24–). First prize – $500.00, Second prize – $250.00 and Third Prize – $100.00. Grand Prize Winner will be selected from among the regional winners. The Grand Prize is a 5 day, 4 night trip to Barbados for four persons, including airfare and accommodations, compliments of the Barbados Tourism Authority, BWIA International, Bougainvillea Beach resort and Sandy Beach Island Resort.

7. All entries must be postmarked by midnight March 31, 1998. Prizes will be awarded by June 30, 1998. Entries must be sent to:

Renaissance Productions Essay Contest
537 Mantua Avenue, Suite 203
Woodbury, New Jersey 08096

8. The contest is void where prohibited by law. Taxes and fees are the responsibility of the winners. Contestants' names may be used for publicity purposes.

Road to Glory

Doctor's Orders

The book you now hold in your hands is the product of much research. I encourage every African American to read this powerful book. Don and Joel have captured the essence of the pain of the black experience in America and have given us a road map to wholeness. You will not exit this gripping book the same way you came in.

I also encourage every non-African American interested in racial reconciliation to read *Return to Glory*. It will enhance their understanding of what people of color deal with on a daily basis.

Julius "Dr. J." Erving
Cherry Hill, New Jersey

PART I – THE BLACK MAN:
HIS PAST RESTORED / HIS PRESENT FACED
HIS FUTURE HOPE DEFINED

1 | The Greatest Rip-Off of All Time

The glory days of boxing in the Heavyweight Division. I still remember it well. One event in particular I will never forget. A great African American boxer by the name of Muhammad Ali stuns the sporting world.

It's 1974. The "Rumble in the Jungle." Everyone in the jam-packed stadium in Zaire, Africa, is sitting on the edge of history. Ali is a 4-to-1 underdog. Foreman seems invincible. Some are thinking Ali will be lucky to escape with his life.

Eight tension-filled rounds later, the place flips out. The upset happens. Ending the fierce battle with a crushing right, Ali defeats George Foreman by a knockout! During the post-fight interview, Ali looks into the camera, proclaiming to the world, "I am the greatest of alll tiiime!" He was some fighter. I think he is deserving of the title, "The Greatest!" He declared it many times and then backed it up with his unshakable mental toughness, with his trademark "Rope-A-Dope," and with his fists. I respect that.

Other fight fans think Mike Tyson, Joe Louis, Joe Frazier or others deserve the title. So, as you can imagine, I have been in a couple of lively discussions over the years on who truly deserves to be called "The Greatest."

The greatest? Let's turn a sharp corner here. How about the greatest rip-off of all time? What's that all about? The book you hold in your hands contains research exposing what we (Don and Joel) believe to be one of the greatest rip-offs of all time. Like the greatest in boxing, this is a hotly debated topic.

We warn you. This is a challenging, probing book. Study it carefully. You may read stuff you've never heard or considered before. You may be rocked by emotions that will land you on your back momentarily. You will be invited to change your way of thinking in areas you may have never explored before. Sometimes the ride may get bumpy. One thing is for sure—you will experience a powerful stirring in your heart. Bottom line: As in most things, you will have to make up your own mind. But all we ask is one thing: Read the **whole** book before you make up your mind.

The title of this chapter begs the question: Who got ripped off? Would you believe that YOU did? That's right. People who rip off folk tend to target certain victims. In a larger sense, the victim we're talking about is an entire race—black people all over the world.

But what was stolen? Important question. The missing item is a large segment of their past, a glorious past—an ancient history that belongs to them but which was craftily snatched and given to others.

To remove the legacy of an entire race from the minds of the masses is a tremendous act of deception. We call it "the greatest rip-off of all time."

RECLAIMING STOLEN GOODS

About two years ago, I (Don) was awakened to the truth of the glorious past of my people. I discovered some things that blew my mind. In my research, I unearthed the surprising truth that the first and greatest civilizations designed by humans were the inventions of the black man. The genius and creativity of black people go back to the dawn of human history.

How did school treat you? Did somebody say you couldn't be a scientist, engineer, or author of books? I hope not, because your ancestors were the first to invent science, engineering, and writing. But that's not all. Blacks were also the first to discover medicine, architecture, astronomy, engineering, agriculture, banking systems, and much more.

Instead of being a debtor to humanity, black people were the fountain, the very spring, from which civilization as we know it has flowed.

Mind boggling, isn't it? If you are like me, the first time you hear it, it's easy to be skeptical. In fact, you may be dealing with some serious doubt right now. *I simply don't believe this. This is just another form of African American propaganda. These guys are trying to pump up the sagging self-esteem of black readers.*

As an African American you may have been so brain-washed by

white-controlled educational systems in this country that it is difficult for you to accept the truth. Hang tough, because we are going to pile the evidence right before your very eyes.

We are aware that mental roadblocks keep some readers from seeing the truth. Prepare to have your mind blown. We will spend some time laying down the evidence revealing your past glory. We will also describe the reason for the black man's fall from such a high pinnacle. Then, the good news: God's plan for a majestic "Return to Glory."

Before attempting this project, we read a lot of books and did a lot of research on this and related subjects. Later on you will be meeting some of the many black brothers we interviewed. They have a lot of insights regarding this area. Many people (black and white) are indirectly involved in this book. To them we are indebted, and to them we will always be grateful.

THE TRUTH WILL ALWAYS RISE

Someone once said, "The truth, crushed to the ground, will always raise its head."[1] Thank God that this is happening in this generation. What you are reading in this book about black studies is part of a movement of God. Professors and scholars are revealing the truth about ancient black history. Black preachers across North America are talking about the marvelous way God used black folk in the Bible.

Congratulations! If you have gotten this far, you probably are a seeker after truth. You can now avail yourself of several other books on this great subject. It is our hope that *Return to Glory* will encourage you to get busy with your own study.

As you read, some questions and reactions will begin to percolate in your head and heart. Don't worry. When this happens, you are joining the company of many before you who have asked similar questions. Why would anybody purposely distort the history of my people? What's the point? What do I do with the anger I feel churning in the pit of my stomach? What's up with the cover-up? What can I do to correct this deception?

In addressing these and other important questions, we (Don and Joel) will be like a well-balanced offensive machine. Working on the outside, I (Don) will be on the court busting down lies and deception with sweet jumpers from 3-point land. I want to hear you shouting and cheering as the ball hits nothing but net.

My Christian brother, Joel, will be waiting anxiously as we take the game into the trenches. He'll be banging the boards, posting up, and rejecting garbage as he helps us through the difficult struggles on our return to glory.

Are you ready for us to take you on a journey? Let's jump into the time machine. We're going beyond roots. Beyond Kunta Kinte. You are about to meet some serious homeboys. Homeboys you will never forget.

Time Out

1. Think back on the statement about blacks being the fountain, the very spring, from which civilization as we know it has flowed. What is your immediate internal response as you read this?

2. Do you consider yourself a seeker after truth? Would your closest friends describe you as such? Why?

3. What are your expectations as you start this book? If you say you have no expectations, why don't you?

4. If you are not of African descent, what are you thinking and feeling at this point?

2 | Homeboys You Will Never Forget

To find out how the homeboys made it big in the world, you must go back to the 'hood. Back to where your old partners hung out. Back to your roots. For the black man that means—ultimately—back to Africa.

Now, I would like to pause at this early juncture for a moment of reflection. I want to ask you a couple of questions to get you thinking. Remember in Chapter 1 when we told you of our discovery that black people invented the earliest civilizations of mankind? Well, if that is true, where would you expect the location of one of the first and greatest civilizations to be? In China? In Japan? In Russia? In North America? On the plains of Europe? How about grand old England?

Some of you are thinking, *No, none of those places.* Well, you've got that right. The location of one of the earliest and greatest civilizations is where the original "boys in the 'hood" hung out. Today it is called Africa. More specifically, the northeast corner of Africa. The location of ancient Egypt.

A SIMPLE GEOGRAPHY LESSON

The ordinary person walking the street often cannot tell you that Egypt is located on the continent of Africa. Some would incorrectly say, "southern Europe." Others would tell you, "the Middle East." The term "Middle East" would be more accurate, but they would miss the truth that Egypt is on the continent of Africa.[1] You see, the term "Middle East" was not in use until it was created by World War II correspondents.[2] Some social commentators feel the creation of the term was to serve one main purpose, to avoid talking about Africa.[3]

In the interest of truth, we will not avoid talking about the great continent. We want to spend some time there. Why? Because as already mentioned, one of the greatest civilizations of antiquity was located on that piece of real estate.

Unlike the common man, there is no confusion today among "educators" as to the location of Egypt. But, as one might expect, there is much confusion on the racial identity of the ancient Egyptian people. Have you watched any movies lately that include segments where ancient Egypt is the location. The place is populated almost exclusively by Europeans. For example, do you think Moses looked like Charlton Heston, as portrayed in the movie "The Ten Commandments?" I seriously doubt it, brother. Well then, who were those Egyptians really?

WHO WERE THE EGYPTIANS?

As I have already hinted, the Egyptians were an African people. Yes, that means they were a black people. Homeboys. Brothers, if you will.

Unfortunately, the black identity of the original Egyptians is one of the best kept secrets in academia. Most people believe the Egyptians were white folk. You should know that this is partly due to the efforts of modern scholars.[4] They have spilled enough ink to fill a lake trying to remove black people from northeast Africa. All by the stroke of a pen.

Now, I can hear somebody asking, *Were there any eye witnesses of the Egyptian people we can turn to?* That would settle it for me. Man, am I glad you asked that question! I have good news for you. We have eyewitnesses of those Egyptian folk who recorded what they saw.

EYEWITNESS TESTIMONY

Let's deal for a moment with the importance of eyewitness accounts. Most investigators, when they want to find the truth about a situation, look hard for eyewitnesses. Eyewitnesses carry the greatest amount of credibility. This principle is widely accepted in our justice system as well.

I'm not sure about your neighborhood, but where I grew up, eyewitness testimony was also very important. One of the best ways to get laughed off the block was to eagerly describe some event, then have it be found out you weren't even there.

Let me sketch a typical neighborhood situation. I believe this will help illustrate the point of this section. Five guys and I are standing on the street corner. We're hanging out, talking, laughing, and joking around. All of sudden, a boy I will call Stevey comes from around the corner and jumps into the middle of us, obviously very excited.

"I knew they were going to get into it sooner or later," Stevey exclaims. "It finally happened. Little Tommy was running off at the mouth again. He was arguing with Leroy about something jive. At some point, Tommy got really ticked off at something Leroy said. Then he began saying nasty things about Leroy's mom. Before you knew it, bip!!! Leroy hit him with a left jab to the jaw. Then, wap!!! Up side the head with a right. Little Tommy was getting fired up bad. Then, out of the blue, baaaammmmmm!!! Little Tommy hit Leroy with a left hook to the chin and boom!!! Leroy went down."

Stevey now pauses, breathing a little heavy after acting all this out. He concludes, "Fight was over, man. All over."

We were all watching him wide eyed and with total attention. Then one of the brothers just had to ask a simple question, "Hey, Stevey, were you there?!!!"

Stevey, now looking a little sheepish, responds, "No, I heard about it."

Everybody cracks up laughing, "Fool, you come up here all loud, throwin' punches in the air, huffin' and puffin' and carryin' on, talkin' 'bout I heard about it."

"Ha!" chimed in another one of the brothers.

Embarrassing. Talking big but saw nothing. We wanted to get the real deal on that neighborhood episode from somebody who actually saw it.

If you're like me, you don't want to be caught doing what Stevey did. And if you happen to get caught doing it, you definitely don't want your story to contradict what the eyewitnesses say. Then the boys might not only call you a fool, but a lying fool, to boot.

Thankfully, in the area of Egyptian history, we have the recorded testimony of eyewitnesses. Unlike my man Stevey, they can tell you what they saw with their own eyes. And they have something important to say about the racial identity of the ancient Egyptians. You will find that eyewitnesses of ancient Egypt tell you straight up that the Egyptians were black.

HERODOTUS

The first eyewitness we will call to the floor is an ancient (white) Greek historian by the name of Herodotus. He is recognized by many as the first great historian. The Father of History. Somewhere around 457-450 B.C. he wrote in *The Histories* that: "The Colchians, Ethiopians and Egyptians have thick lips, broad nose, woolly hair and they are burnt of skin."[5] (Can you imagine someone with that description in Mississippi, in the 1940s, demanding to sit in the front of the bus?)

Why does this great historian make the above observation? Well, Herodotus is trying to show readers how black people in what until recently was southern Russia (inhabitants of Colchis) got to that location.[6] He believed they originally came from Africa since the black people of that time lived primarily in Africa. The most commonly known countries there were Egypt and Ethiopia.

So Herodotus makes a simple argument that goes something like this. We know the Egyptians are black. We know the Colchians are black. We also know that the Egyptians passed through Colchis once as a conquering army, during the reign of Sesostris I, around 1900 B.C.[7] Some of the Egyptian soldiers obviously stayed and did not return home.[8] According to Herodotus, that's how black folk got to present day southern Russia.

On another occasion, as Herodotus makes a point concerning the flooding of the Nile,[9] he refers to the blackness of the Egyptians' skin, "And the third proof is that the men of the country are black by reason of the heat."[10] His statement that Egyptians are black with heat has also been used to describe Ethiopians. In fact, the word Ethiopian means "black or burnt face" in Greek.[11]

Let me run by you one more quote from Herodotus. This time, the great historian is making a point about Greek religious symbols. He is trying to show that the symbols come from Egypt. And how does he attempt to prove this? You guessed it. He refers to the black skin of the Egyptians. He then compares their skin to the blackness of the symbols. He writes: "The tale that the dove was black signifies that the woman was Egyptian. . . ."[12] Dr. Diop notes that the black doves here represent two women carried off from Thebes in Egypt, Africa.[13]

DIODORUS OF SICILY

This serves as a nice introduction to our next eyewitness. Diodorus of Sicily, another ancient historian, writes, "They say also that the Egyptians are colonists sent out by the Ethiopians, Osiris having been the leader of the colony. . . . And the larger part of the customs of the Egyptians are, they hold, Ethiopian, the colonists [Egyptians] still preserving their ancient [Ethiopian] manners. For instance, the belief that their kings are gods, the very special attention which they pay to their burials . . . the shapes of their statues and the forms of their letters are Ethiopian."[14]

Interesting! An ancient white scholar quoting the Ethiopians as saying the Egyptians descended from them. Not a word of dispute, on a racial basis, to be sure. Check this out. Two great scholars are revealing something important. They are telling us that the Colchians (blacks in southern Russia), the Egyptians, and the Ethiopians are part of the same race.[15] Namely, they are black, colored, African, Negroes. You pick the term. The ethnic point is the same. There was no argument or confusion about this with the ancients. Why? It is fairly difficult to dispute what everybody can see with their own eyes. That would be like going to Harlem in New York and saying, "No black people live here."

This is only a sample of the eyewitness testimony. Time does not permit us to refer to the ancient writings of Pliny, Tacitus, Julius Africanus, Strabo, St. Augustine, Josephus, and many, many more.[16] They all describe the Africans of Egypt and Ethiopia as having "Thick lips, broad noses, woolly hair, burnt skin. . . ."[17] The evidence can be summed up by one statement made by Gaston Maspero (1846-1916), a more modern white historian. He writes, "By the almost unanimous testimony of ancient historians, they (Egyptians) belonged to an African race which first settled in Ethiopia, on the Middle Nile."[18]

A PICTURE'S WORTH A THOUSAND WORDS

Some of you loved reading about that eyewitness testimony. I know I enjoyed it. But I can hear somebody saying, *Do you have any pictures of the Egyptians?* Man, am I glad you asked that question! I have some good news for you. We not only have pictures in the form of paintings, we also have huge statues to tell you about. In fact, I want to share this with you so badly, I'm going to give these brothers another chapter. Can you handle that? I thought so. Let's do it.

Time Out

1. How important is an eyewitness to you in regard to accepting new information? Why?

2. Of the eyewitness testimony you've read so far, which account impacts you the hardest? Why this one?

3. What emotion, if any, surfaced the most as you were reading? Joy? Sadness? Anger? Hurt? Grief? Or did you experience no emotional response at all?

4. Where do you stand now with regard to your opinion concerning the racial identity of ancient Egyptians? Does this represent a change from when you started this book? Why?

5. If you are not of African descent, how would you answer the four questions above?

3 | Homeboys You Will Never Forget

Just look at that family resemblance! I always find it enjoyable to look at family pictures. I like seeing how some family members resemble their parents and other relatives. It's fun. I'm sure you've heard things like, *His lips and nose are just like Uncle George's, walks like him, too. Or Look at those eyes and that big forehead, just like her Aunt Louise. Or that boy's built up strong and stocky like his ole man.*

WHAT YOU SEE IS WHAT YOU GET

Because of strong family resemblance, stereotypical statements are sometimes made. I've heard some people say, "All black people look alike." I've heard others say, "All white people look alike." We know that such comments are not entirely true. Nevertheless, there are recognizable physical characteristics common within ethnic groups—a sort of family resemblance.

Given this reality, if you went to Egypt and looked at a big statue of one of the people, I have a hunch you could tell the race of that person. Take a look at the statue of Abe Lincoln in Washington, D.C. I wouldn't spend three seconds arguing with someone about his racial identity. You would look up at that face and say, Yes, that's a white man. Not that this method is infallible. But in most cases, you would probably be right, unless there was a high degree of racial mixture.

One of the largest statues in the world is of an Egyptian. Located near Cairo in Egypt, Africa, it is called the Sphinx of Giza. I want to share with you the account of a man who saw it, a famous historian by the name of Count Constantine de Volney. This scholar made a trip to Egypt between 1783 and 1785.[1] He wanted to see things with his own eyes. Count de Volney went up to the Sphinx of Giza and took a look at that beautiful face, serene and full of wisdom. He was looking at a part of

Africa's "family picture album."

The historian had also seen living examples of Africans in his own lifetime—you know, the family of folk who were brought to America as slaves. He must have had sketched in his mind's eye images of the slave ancestors of the African American. So, as he raised his eyes to gaze upon that great Sphinx, he thought and later wrote, "On seeing that head, typically Negro in all its features, I remembered the remarkable passage (of Herodotus). . . . The ancient Egyptians were true Negroes of the same type as all native-born Africans." After commenting in the same passage on the brilliant mind of the Greeks and the genius of the Egyptians, he continues, "Just think that this race of black men, today are slave and the object of scorn . . . the very race to which we owe our arts, sciences, and even the use of speech."[2]

I heard that!!!

But I never heard it in school. Not in elementary school, not in middle school, not in high school, and not in college. Listen to what the scholar is saying. The Negro, who he openly admits is the object of efforts to "prove" his inferiority, is the inventor of civilization. To the black man of Africa, Europe owes its education. It is from the black man that the European learned art. It is from the black man that he learned science. It is from the black man that he learned the use of speech.

Scholar Baron V. Denon confirmed Count de Volney's views in his book, *Journey and Travels in Egypt and Assyria*.[3] He, too, spoke of the greatness of the Negroes.[4] His hand drawing of the Sphinx of Giza, sketched in 1798, shows us the way the statue looked before it was disfigured.[5] According to eyewitness Baron V. Denon, Napoleon's soldiers blew its nose and lips apart with cannon fodder during the French invasion of Egypt.[6] Only God knows the motivation behind this senseless act of vandalism.

We would do well in America to heed the words of English scholar Joseph McCabe,

> The accident of the predominance of white men in modern times should not . . . persuade us to listen to superficial theories about the innate superiority of the white-skinned man. Four thousand years ago, when civilization was already one or two thousand years old, white men were just a bunch of semi-savages on the outskirts of the civilized world.

If there had been anthropologists in Crete, Egypt, and Babylon, they would have pronounced the white race obviously inferior and might have discoursed learnedly on . . . the glands of colored folk.[7]

The truth of what the English scholar has written can be seen in a statement made by the Romans concerning the Britons, a white-skinned people who lived in present day England. The Romans said that these folk were "too dumb to make slaves of them."[8] Modern history is its own commentary on the stupidity of such statements.

It is not possible in a book of this size and scope to go through a detailed analysis of the archeological evidence available. For a pictorial review, we recommend the following books:

Cheikh Anta Diop's *The African Origin of Civilization* is probably the best single work on this aspect of African history. On the front cover there is pictured a sculpture of the Egyptian Pharaoh Tuthmosis III, the son of a Sudanese woman and founder of the 18th Dynasty.[9] I'm sure somebody will say when they see that picture, almost without thinking, *That brother looks just like so-and-so in my family.* (That is, if you have black folk in your family.)

Ivan Van Sertima's books, *Egypt Revisited* and *Egypt: Child of Africa*, contain an impressive array of photographs, showcasing the Negro identity of Egypt's greatest rulers.

This is only a sample, but you will find these works to be very informative and a good place to start.

HOMEBOY HIGHLIGHTS OF FIRSTS

Based on the testimony of ancient and more recent eyewitnesses, we now know who the Egyptians were. With that achieved, we should take a look at some of their accomplishments. Let's approach it like checking out a highlight film. We will focus our attention on the big moments when the brothers were the people who came in first. I call it Homeboy Highlights of Firsts.

A good place to start would be the beginning of civilization. Egypt developed into a nation around 3200 B.C. A native African, a homeboy from Ethiopia, known by the Greeks as Menes, succeeded in conquering all of Egypt. In triumph, he established the First Dynasty (powerful family of rulers who maintain power for a long time). However, this great black man and his people did more than establish the First Dynasty.

Here, in Africa, we have an impressive list of firsts. These black people created the first written records; the first monumental structures; the first architecture; the first systematic removal of metals from the earth; the first copper mines; the first use of beds, tables, and chairs.[10] In short, they established the "beginning of civilization."[11]

During the Third and Fourth African Dynasties (2780-2270 B.C.), Egypt reached the "peak (of its) material and artistic glory."[12] This age, for example, saw the creation of the great pyramids of Giza.[13] The advanced mathematical, engineering, and architectural know-how involved is so impressive that it even amazes modern astronomers and mathematicians. The precision of the structures alone earned them the status of one of the seven wonders of the world.[14] In addition, painting and art were highly developed by the Fourth Dynasty.[15]

During this same period, a black brother by the name of Imhotep, architect of the first step pyramid, dabbled in medicine.[16] A man of many talents, he was deified before his death as the "Great God of Medicine."[17] This lofty title was given to him by Africans and Europeans.[18] He invented this science 1500 years before Hippocrates of Greece, the so-called "Father of Medicine," was even born.[19]

COME ON, SOMEBODY!

In many black churches, preaching is a two-way communication exercise. It's not like a classroom lecture. Congregational worship doesn't stop when the singing stops. It continues with the preaching of the Word. The congregation often responds during the sermon with an "Amen," or "Praise the Lord," or "Hallelujah."

When the preacher reveals an important truth, he will expect that "Amen" in response. Sometimes, when he reveals a truth that some folk are reluctant to admit, at least publicly, there is silence. When that happens, he may say, "Come on, somebody!" That usually will work in bringing somebody out in the open with an affirming, "Amen, Brother" or an encouraging, "Preach the Word, Pastor!"

So far, you have heard compelling evidence on the true racial identity of the ancient Egyptians. Eyewitness evidence. Archeological and anthropological evidence. And soon, biblical evidence. Evidence that would even impress my man Stevey back on the block.

Yes, the Egyptians were some serious brothers, "Homeboys You Will Never Forget." Wouldn't you agree? Come on, Somebody!!!

Time Out

1. What were you taught in school about black history that stands out the most? Has this had any impact on your life? How about your view of yourself, your view of your race, of other people?

2. How does knowing that your black ancestors were the founders of great civilizations make you feel?

3. Make a list of four of the accomplishments of the Egyptians that you are the most proud of. Why did you pick these four?

4. Why is it important to know about your past?

5. If you are not of African descent, how did the teaching of black history in school affect your view of black people? How about your view of yourself and your view of your race?

4 | What's God Got to Do With It?

Chapters 2 and 3 took us on some trip—a remarkable visit with a remarkable people. Our ancient ancestors from the Nile River Valley had the *baddest* civilization on the planet. They dominated for many years. They actually lasted longer as a power than most, if not all, other great civilizations. But they fell, didn't they? Why? Let's talk about it.

THIS IS MY PLANET

Do you remember seeing the TV commercial where a superstar athlete concludes the advertisement by saying, "This is my planet"? In some respects, for the first 2,000 years of recorded human history, black people could almost make that boast. Even the Word of God said the Ethiopian (black man) was "feared far and wide" (Isaiah 18:1, 2) and that his power was "without limit" (Nahum 3:9).

These African nations, once dominating the world, are now near the bottom in prestige and power. Is this surprising? Actually the fall of great nations is quite common. Remember Rome? The Roman legions were once feared. They had the *baddest* army on earth. Rome, as you know, is a city in Italy. Have you heard much about the military might of Italy lately? No, I didn't think so. Have you heard much about the dominance of Greece in world affairs lately? No, I didn't think so. Talking about decline and fall, how about going backward? Ever hear of the Middle Ages? Things got so bad the historians called it the dark ages. From the glory of Rome and Greece to the backwardness of the middle ages—think about it.[1] That dismal stretch of world history clung to Europe like a cheap suit for over a thousand years (from 300 to 1475 A.D.).[2]

I could give you a whole list of nations and empires throughout history that fit the same pattern. They rise, and then they fall.

No, This Is His Planet

As I'm sure you noticed, the chapter title sounds a lot like, "What's love got to do with it?" as sung by Tina Turner in her hit release of some years ago. While the questions sound similar, the answers are quite different. Carnal human love can be a "second hand emotion," as Tina points out. But God is the source of all true love. He is love, declares the Bible (1 John 4:16). And God is the source of all power. He has all power in His hand.

What's God got to do with it? Everything. It is God Almighty who allows a nation to rise and then takes a nation down. He is the only one who can say, "This is my planet," and be legit when He says it. Nations, empires, peoples, and tribes are in His hand. He defines the limits of their habitations and the extent of their power.

What happened to black civilization? Let's cut to the chase. There weren't enough white people on this earth to bring the black man down. The answer to the rise and fall of the nations—black, white, or yellow is rooted in God, not man.

Speak to Me, Lord

How do I find God's answer? How do I get His perspective and His role straight in my mind? Only one way. You have to go to the manufacturer's handbook. It's called the Bible. This is God's primary way of communicating with mankind. History is, in reality, *His story.* "Yeah, I heard that before. But does the Bible have anything to say about black people in particular? Are we in the Bible?" Good question, brothers. Let me assure you of this. You are in the Bible. Big time!

Black Presence in the Bible

The white man's book. The Muslims' favorite put down line for Christianity. Whoever told you the Bible is the white man's book is misinformed or, worse, trying to deceive you. As Father Clarence Williams says, "The Bible is a treasury of black history."[3] We believe it to be a completely dependable source for finding truth on history, culture, ethnology (race), and more. The Bible can "hold its own" against any other ancient record.[4] In short, we believe the Bible is the inspired Word of God. It is the final word on all subjects where it speaks as an authority.

It's time to dig into the book. In its pages we find our unique position in God's program. But before we dig out the truth about black folk in the Bible, we need to ensure that we have the proper tools. You can't do the job right without the right equipment.

LESSONS FROM A BAD HAIRCUT

Have you ever seen one of those home barber kits? When I was a young boy my father was my barber. To save some money, he'd cut my hair with this trimmer he bought. To keep things even and not to take too much hair off, the trimmer had attachable guards. I'll never forget the last haircut he gave me. The attachment he used was defective. I discovered this early on in the process. He'd be buzzing along, and then he'd nick me. "No problem, Son. I just need to cut a little more off to make it even," my father said.

"Okay, Pop."

A minute later, "Sorry, Son." Another nick. "Got to take a little more off to make it even."

"What's going on, Dad," I questioned. I was really getting concerned now. "No problem. Everything is under control," he assured me.

To make a long story short, he got it even all right. I ended up bald headed. Baldness wasn't in style when I was eleven years old. Trying to hide my shameful haircut until my hair grew back was not an easy thing to do. Improper tools. My dad never cut my hair again. That was okay with him. Afros were coming into style about that time. He wouldn't have been able to trim my bush right, anyway.

That event taught me something. To do a job right, you need the right tools. It's worth the effort to get the right equipment together. In searching for blacks in the Bible, we need the proper methods, or tools, to do the job right. Let's spend the effort in pulling them together.

ASSEMBLING THE TOOLS

Rev. Walter Arthur McCray in his *Black Presence in the Bible* provides a helpful road map for finding black people in the scriptures. One method he explains is through the use of names and adjectives.[5] Names in the Bible, Rev. McCray notes, are usually loaded with meaning. They were used to describe something about a person. It could be a character trait or skin color.[6]

Think of it this way. Biblical names are similar to how we use nick-names.[7] This is especially true when referring to someone's national or ethnic origin.[8] Here are some examples from Rev. McCray's book:

"Kedar" in the Bible means "very black."[9] "Phinehas" means "the Negro" or "the Nubian."[10] "Cush," which means "black," identifies a people or a nation; and "Ham" signifies "black."[11]

BLACK IS THE ROOT, SO IS THE FRUIT[12]

Another tool for the tool bag is to look at ancestors, or family trees, of people.[13] This is simple. If a person's father or grandfather is black, then the person is black. Through this easy method we discover that a black man wrote one of the books of the Bible. Really? What book? The old testament book Zephaniah. In chapter one, verse one, of the book, the black prophet tells us his father's name is Cushi. Cushi means "black."

BEFORE COLOR PREJUDICE

During ancient times there was no such thing as color prejudice.[14] You won't find it in the Bible. It's hard for us to imagine this, since our culture is saturated with this kind of racism. People identified themselves as black, or were identified as black, just as a statement of fact. Rev. McCray points out, for example, that black people in Scripture referred to themselves as black as a statement of fact, value, and beauty.[15] In the Song of Solomon we find the Shulamite woman saying, "I am black and beautiful."[16]

Another example would be the prophet Jeremiah's reference to black people. He simply makes a statement of fact concerning their skin color. He asks, "Can the Ethiopian change his skin. . . ?" Jeremiah 13:23).[17]

THE KEY THAT UNLOCKS THE DOOR

Genesis 10:1-32 contains the key passage concerning the rise of nations and groups recognizable today.[18] It's called the Table of Nations. Scholars have wasted much effort searching for a document more accurate.[19] The majority of people found in the world can be traced to a person or group found in this Table.[20] Thus the black man's family tree can be found in these verses. It shows our ancestors, where they lived, and their political affiliations.[21]

Remember those homeboys we met in chapters 2 and 3? Sure you do. They're unforgettable. We're going to bump into them again in Genesis 10. We'll also meet some other brothers in Isaiah 18 who are likewise hard to forget. We'll get acquainted with them very soon.

FASTEN YOUR SEAT BELTS

The next chapter is going to be quite a ride. If you're faint of heart, better get off now. Some of what you read will be controversial. But it will be true to the Bible. Straight up exposition. Speaking the truth. Letting the chips fall where they may.

The right equipment has now been assembled. We're ready to mine the truth of God's Word for His message to our people. Are you ready? Let's get busy.

Time Out

1. Were you surprised to read that the Bible has so much to say about black folk? Does this affect the way you view the Bible? Why?

2. How does the truth that God is in control of nations impact your view of God? Does the current plight of the black man cause you to blame God or make you angry with Him? Why or why not?

3. Read Genesis 10:1-32. List the sons of Noah and Ham.

4. Define the meanings of the following words: Kedar, Phinehas, Cush, Ham.

5. If you are not of African descent, what thoughts and emotions did you have as you read about the black presence in the Bible? Does this affect your view of black people or the Bible in any way? Why?

5 | They Can Dance, Too

Thank God for His servants, like black preacher and counselor, Dr. Clarence Walker. And thank God for the invention of cassette players and tapes that aid in spreading their messages. Why am I so thankful? I can't wait to tell you. It started when a small group of five black men were sitting around the kitchen table. We had just finished a dynamite breakfast, but that wasn't our main reason for being there. We were gathered together for the purpose of supporting each other in our quest to be godly men.

The center of our attention that fateful morning was a message by Dr. Walker. His topic was "AFRO-ESCHATOLOGY." We listened intently to the cassette recording of that powerful sermon. We were gripped by what he had to say. As I remember, we started fumbling for our Bibles as the message progressed. "Find it yet?" "Okay, got it." We read along. "Yeah, it's there all right." The passage under examination was Isaiah 18.

A PROPHETIC MESSAGE

"This is a prophetic message especially for black people in the last day."[1] Beginning with these introductory remarks, Dr. Walker pointed out that you would not find this teaching among famous prophecy teachers in evangelical Christendom. In my own research on Isaiah 18, I found Bible commentators to be somewhat confusing. Sadly, they did more dancing than Mr. Bo-Jangles. The reason? Apparently to side step the clear meaning of this important text. And you thought scholars didn't dance!

STICK TO THE BIBLE

There is nothing spooky about what you're going to read in the next four chapters. We will show, through a straightforward exposition of the text, God's plan for black people. We will prove, black brothers, that you are indeed in the Book.

With the aid of the Holy Spirit, we will bring together three separate prophecies concerning black people: Zephaniah 3:10, Isaiah 18, and Psalm 68:31.[2]

First, let's pause for a moment. I'm going to request something of you. Please get a Bible. I want you to follow me verse by verse with this book and the Bible at your side. What translation? I'll be reading and quoting from the New King James Version. The New International Version (NIV) and the New American Standard (NAS) are some other translations that you can use. Why the fuss about getting a Bible? I'll let you know later. My only advice to you now is to keep your dancing shoes handy.

PUT YOUR READING GLASSES ON

It's time for a little reading. Are you ready? Turn to Zephaniah 3:10. It says, "From beyond the rivers of Ethiopia (read Cushite Sudanese Africa), My worshipers, My dispersed ones, will bring My offerings." Underline the word *worshipers*. God is foretelling that beyond the rivers of Cushite Sudanese Africa, born-again black folk will bring offerings to Him. From a family tree perspective, their number will include Christians who have Jewish blood in them.

You mean there are black people who are also Jews? Absolutely. Jewishness (physically not spiritually) is about a family ancestry, not a color. It's really quite simple to understand. After the destruction of the Jewish temple by the Romans in 70 A.D. the Jews dispersed to various parts of the world. Some fled to Africa as well as to Asia, and some were taken to Europe as slaves.[3]

If a people spent hundreds of years on the predominantly white continent of Europe, guess what would happen? Through intermarriage with Europeans, their descendants would get lighter and lighter. If they fled to Africa and spent hundreds of years on that continent, guess what would happen? Their descendants through intermarriage with the people of that area would be dark.

Here is a little-known fact that illustrates the point. The ancient historians thought the original Jews were black folk.[4] Such was the opinion of Flavius Josephus, Plutarch, Tacitus, and others.[5] They taught that the Jews were Egyptians and Ethiopians who were driven out of Egypt and later settled in Canaan.[6]

When you realize the Jews were only seventy people when they first went to Africa, lived there for 430 years, and came out three million strong, then it's not very surprising. If they weren't black when they first went to Africa, many—if not most—would've been black by the time they left under Moses.[7]

Would you like a more recent example? Consider the fascinating Falasha Jews. They are black people who were cut off from all other Jews, yet maintained Judaism down through the centuries. Many have migrated to Israel in recent years.

Okay, let's summarize. Zephaniah 3:10 is teaching us that a black people will bring an offering to God in the last days. He calls these black children "My worshipers."

Keep Your Reading Glasses On

Are you still with me? Let's read Isaiah 18:1 and 2.

> Woe to the land shadowed with buzzing wings, which is beyond the rivers of Ethiopia [remember what we learned about names in the last chapter], which sends ambassadors by the sea even in vessels of reed on the waters. Go, swift messengers, to a nation tall and smooth of skin, to a people, terrible from their beginning onward, a nation powerful and treading down; whose land the rivers divide.

Let's see if we can make it plain. The phrase "buzzing wings" is probably a description of locusts in Africa.[8] Remember, Ethiopia means black in Scripture. In this verse, it's referring to a place. Namely, Cushite Sudanese Africa. The ambassadors that are sent in verse 2, may be referring to messengers going to Israel to form an alliance against Assyria.[9] This nation was an emerging power at the time. Israel eventually fell to them in 722 B.C.

It's time for me to give you your first quiz. Did "homeboys" sit on pharaoh's throne at the time the prophet Isaiah was writing this? All right! You get an A+. On the throne were some awesome black brothers from Nubia/Ethiopia, founders of the 25th Dynasty of Egypt. Even your more prejudiced modern scholars didn't try to reclassify these brothers. Couldn't find any wiggle room.

One modern scholar properly admitted that Taharqa, the first pharaoh of this Dynasty, was a *Negro*. He writes, "The throne of Egypt was occupied by a Negro king from Ethiopia."[10] I hesitate to include another comment from a modern scholar about this 25th Dynasty. But I'm going to do it because it's important for you to understand to what extent racism has poisoned so-called "scholarship". Especially scholarship involving black folk.

Scholar Arthur Weigall in referring to Piankhi, predecessor of Taharqa, called him "the most famous of the 'nigger kings.'"[11] Shocked aren't you? So was I. Most aren't as direct. But as you will see, racism played far too big a role in the writing of black and African history.

There is no place for racism in true scholarship or any place else for that matter. Enough said. Let's go back to the brothers. These black kings accomplished something that seemed impossible at the time.[12] They conquered, united, and ruled all of Egypt. Their reign proved to be the final burning of the flame of Egyptian glory.

LATER HAS NOW ARRIVED

Remember earlier when I made the fuss about getting a Bible? I said I'd explain why later. Guess what? Later has arrived. In Isaiah 18:2, we read "to a nation tall. . . ." Now hold on a minute. Are you ready for this? Historically, many Bible scholars have misinterpreted and wrongly translated this passage.[13]

I'll cover with you the most common errors you are likely to run into. For example, some commentators read Isaiah 18:2 this way ". . . to a nation scattered." If I say *scattered* to you, what images do you see?[14] Here are some: *disorganized, confused, running afraid with no direction.* All negative. The original word actually means "tall, extended, stretched out, and made long."[15] My New King James Version, the NIV, the Living Bible paraphrase, and the NAS all translate the word *tall.* That's what it means. How do you get *scattered* out of that?[16] Frankly, it's an inaccurate translation. It doesn't even do justice to the context. If you think that's bad, there's more.

In that very same verse we read ". . . to a nation tall and smooth skinned. . . ." The Hebrew word is "Mârat."[17] Here we go again. Historically, many scholars have translated that same word *stripped* and *peeled.* It sounds like these translators/interpreters were thinking about a banana or maybe an orange. When you read that, what's the image you get? I won't even go into it. The images will be negative.

The word actually means *polished* and *furbished*.[18] Listen carefully, this is good. It means "polished to the point where all the impurities have been removed."[19] Dr. Walker thinks God is referring to the melanin in black people's skin. You know what God is expressing to you here? When He created you, black brothers, He polished you until all of the impurities were gone.[20] This is so your skin would shine real pretty. God is bringing focus to the fact that you are beautifully and wonderfully made.

Brothers, ever notice how a 55-year-old black woman can look 10 to 15 years younger than her age? The sisters seem to age more gracefully. That's due in part to the melanin in the skin. That's something to praise the Lord about isn't it? Go ahead, it's all right.[21]

SOMETHIN' IN THE MILK AIN'T CLEAN

God has just made reference to the black man's physical appearance. Tall and smooth-skinned. And you wondered how those NBA ballplayers got so tall. Now you know. Those brothers are Cushites. Let's keep reading, ". . .to a people terrible from their beginning onward, a nation powerful and treading down (read conquering)." God says these people were so awesome that they were respected all over the known world. They were a powerful and conquering people. Now let me show you what I've found among some *scholars*. They read, "It is a nation that has been terrible and is now . . . meted out and trodden down. . . ."[22] We have a very different meaning don't we? In the Bible text we read the Cushites are powerful and conquering. Some of those commentators made it look like these folk are bad off. Stripped and peeled like a banana, and getting beat up!

It appears to me that racism may have entered into the picture when the scholars translated these verses. This would support a comment made by Bishop Alfred G. Dunston concerning biblical scholarship. In his book, *The Black Man in the Old Testament and Its World*, Dunston writes, "Since the opening years of the sixteenth century, Christian biblical scholarship has been the ally of racism, sometimes deliberately and sometimes unconsciously."[23]

What we have just reviewed with you is very painful. But it needed to be said. In biblical studies, the Hebrew and Greek scholarship can be suspect in certain places. Dr. Walker points out that since the Bible was written in Hebrew and Greek, you can get misled relying on middle men. Not that you have to be a scholar to read the Bible. But it doesn't hurt to have some serious support materials. So, brothers, get yourself a good Hebrew and Greek dictionary if you don't have one. When it comes to the treatment of our people in scholarly works, you need to do your own digging sometimes. But that's good. Because God loves for us to diligently study His precious Word (See 2 Tim. 2:15).

SURPRISED BY THE TRUTH

Surprised? Maybe even shocked? That was the feeling I had when I first read that the Cushite (black man) was "terrible from the beginning onward" and "a nation powerful and treading down." When I graduated from school, I was left with the impression that all black folks did in Africa was run around in grass skirts with bones in their noses. When I finally learned the truth about our history, I had some questions that needed to be answered.

Here is one. How is it that God described these people as so awesome when most educators downplay or ignore them? As one of my old friends used to say, "Somethin' in the milk ain't clean." The Bible itself sheds some light on this subject and answers much of my question. If you look at what the Scriptures say about the Cushite in other parts of the Bible, it becomes clear why Isaiah 18:1, 2 is written this way.

Listen to this. The Bible records throughout its pages the early greatness of the black man. Don't that beat all! The so-called "white man's book" turns out to be the very record that preserves the truth about the black man's glory. Thank God for His Word! Let's take our stand on the Bible. As an ancient record of peoples, it is without equal. For those of us who are Christians, it rises even above that. For us, it's the Word of the living God.

Back in chapter 4 we made reference to the Table of Nations in Genesis chapter 10. Prepare to take a look into that critical historical document in the next chapter. We have a few more nuggets of truth to dig up for our people. I hope you're not tired. We're not even warmed up yet. Maybe we'll break a little sweat in the next chapter. Man, there's nothing like a good spiritual workout in the Word of God. Oh, by the way. Don't forget your tool bag. You're going to need it.

Time Out

1. Has this chapter inspired you to study the Bible?

2. Are you in some kind of Bible study? If not, commit to attending a Sunday school program and/or Bible study each week. Make sure you carry your Bible along, and read for yourself.

3. Why is it important to read along in the Bible with a Bible teacher, and to study the Scriptures for yourself?

4. God's description of the black man is very impressive. What thoughts did you have as you contemplated God's description of black folk?

5. If you are not of African descent, how did reading God's description of the black man impact you? Why? Has this chapter inspired you to study the Bible?

6 | Too Legit to Quit

The Cushite. "Terrible from the beginning" (Isaiah 18:2). When the Bible says *terrible* here, it does not mean *morally wrong*. "The term refers to their accomplishments," explains Dr. Walker. It would be like saying they were *awesome* from the beginning. Such is the testimony of the Word of God.

Wouldn't you like to know what these brothers were up to in the beginning? To find out, we will turn our attention to the Table of Nations in Genesis 10. We'll begin our digging expedition by starting with the listing of Noah's three sons (Gen. 10:1). Why there? "Because," as renowned Bible teacher Dr. Tony Evans points out, "all humanity had its origins in the three sons of Noah (Gen. 9:18-19; Acts 17:26)."[1] This makes the Table the proper place to begin for identifying a people's ethnic/racial background.[2]

NAMES THAT SPEAK

After the great flood that destroyed nearly all of mankind, only eight humans survived. They were Noah, his wife, their three sons, and the sons' wives. God protected them in the great ark He had instructed Noah to build in preparation for the flood.

The names of Noah's three sons were Shem, Ham, and Japheth. Let's begin with Japheth. The name Japheth is interpreted *bright* or *fair* in the Hebrew.[3] Shem means "dusky or olive-colored."[4] Ham signifies "dark or black."[5] By identifying the meaning of Japheth's name and following the habitations of his descendants, you can identify the race he fathered. This pattern, which we will apply to the other names, will help us to trace all the peoples that are on the earth today.

By applying this method, we know that Japheth is the originator of the Caucasians, or white folk.[6] Shem is the originator of the Semites, or Arabic and Hebrew peoples.[7] Ham is the originator of black folk.[8] It is interesting to note that the Bible calls Egypt, Africa, "the land of Ham" (Psalm 78:51).

The purpose of this study is to find the black folk. How will we do that? Just testing you. As you now know, we will have to trace the descendants of Ham. Ham had four sons (Gen. 10:6): Cush, Mizraim, Put, and Canaan. Cush was the father of the Ethiopian people.[9] This is proven by the fact that the Bible uses both Cush and Ethiopia to identify the same place and or people.[10] Cush is the Hebrew word for *black*.[11] Ethiopia is the Greek word meaning *black face.*[12]

Mizraim is the father of the Egyptian people. Put is the father of the Libyans; and Canaan, the father of the Canaanites. As Hamites, all of these people were black.

Rev. McCray points out that a causal reading will reveal that Genesis 10 devotes more space to black people than to any other group (this is especially true of Cush).[13] For example, the verses dealing with Japheth and his descendants are four. Shem and his descendants are dealt with in eleven verses. Ham and his descendants are addressed in fifteen verses.[14] Rev. McCray maintains further that this shows that black people had a position of power, prestige, and dominance in early civilization.[15] It also suggests that the black man played a key role in the outworking of God's purposes in the world.[16]

WHEN A BLACK MAN WAS PRESIDENT

The first great ruler of the world was a man named Nimrod. In a sense, he was president of planet earth. Guess who his daddy was? Cush was his name (Gen. 10:8). D. Alexander Hislop, a renowned European scholar, makes a very informative comment about Nimrod and his father. In his book, *Two Babylons,* he writes, "Now Nimrod, as the son of Cush, was black, in other words, a Negro."[17] He further comments that all ancient and classical art pictured Nimrod as a Negro.[18] This extrabiblical evidence is consistent with the Bible's identification of this great historical figure.

The Scriptures declare this black man to be "a mighty hunter before the Lord." At this time in man's history, an apparent threat to human safety existed. The source of the problem was wild beasts in some fashion. Nimrod, a very gifted hunter, provided for the protection of the community. He was a liberator and a freedom fighter for all humanity.[19]

His physical talents were obviously great.

Rev. McCray argues that Nimrod's courage in this endeavor was attributed to his relationship with God. We know this by the phrase "before the Lord." Here we see the real source behind his success. He was a spiritual man.

It is a little-known fact that ancient people had a high regard for the spirituality of the darker races.[20] The great ancient poet Homer, speaks of the "blameless Ethiopian."[21] He explains that these black people were the only humans regarded by the gods as being fit for high spiritual positions (Olympian divinities).[22] Another example would be from an ancient by the name of Lucius.[23] He was a skeptical follower of his pagan religion and upset with the gods.[24] His reason? The gods didn't answer the prayers of Europeans because they were always with the Ethiopians.[25] I know what some of you are thinking right about now. *Man, how times have changed!*

Although many of the above statements spring from pagan religions, they reflect the high regard ancients had for the black man. Did Nimrod do anything else? Let's be serious. Nimrod, in addition to other talents, possessed great intellectual, political, and organizational genius.[26] The brother founded great cities and built civilizations. The Bible records that Nimrod built his kingdom in the "land of Shinar," also know by historians as Sumer (Gen. 10:10; 11:2).

Before examining his kingdoms, I need to take a brief time out. You need to know something that's gone on in scholarly circles about these civilizations. There has been a debate about which civilization came first. The one founded by Nimrod in the "land of Shinar" or the Egyptian? Up to this point, archaeology would support the Egyptian as being first.[27] If you will recall, in most instances when I referred to Egypt, I mentioned it as one of the first. Now you know why. These two great civilizations appear on the scene fairly close together. At least that's what the evidence indicates from ancient records.

It really doesn't matter much. In either case, both of the civilizations were founded by black folk. That's why you may find some similarities in Egyptian and Mesopotamian civilizations. My own opinion is that black people established the first civilization in Mesopotamia and then migrated to Africa where they did some more building. This seems to fit the Bible's post-flood chronology better. One thing is for sure, those black brothers were very, very busy!

WHEN EQUAL OPPORTUNITY WAS MORE THAN A SLOGAN

As I mentioned in an earlier chapter, there was no such thing as color prejudice in ancient times. That particular malady awaited the emergence of western civilization. In addition, soon after the flood, no one had an advantage over anyone else. In fact, mankind wanted to live in harmony and remain close together. Oddly enough, this formed part of a serious problem. I'll get to that issue a little later.

But for now, let's return to brother Nimrod. As the first world ruler, he built his kingdom in the "land of Shinar." Let's review some facts about this place called Shinar, facts that Dwight McKissic highlighted so aptly in *Beyond Roots:*

FACT NUMBER 1: This region was inhabited mainly by black folk. Renowned Bible scholar Merrill F. Unger states, "Southern Mesopotamia was the original home of Hamitic Cushites." R. K. Harrison, another highly respected white scholar, informs us that a "swarthy (black), non-Semitic group (with) superior intellectual" qualities lived in Sumer.[28]

FACT NUMBER 2: When describing themselves, the people of Shinar often made reference to their blackness.[29] Dr. Custance, a Ph. D. anthropologist, explains that this was a reference to their skin color.[30]

Remember how much I like pictures? Well, these Sumerian brothers left statues behind like their Egyptian kinfolk. They were kind of picky about the stone they used. The Sumerians loved their blackness so much they "consistently chose very dark, preferably black, stone" for the sculptures they made of their leaders.[31]

There's an old Sumerian legend. "What became of the black people of Sumer?" the traveler asked the old man. "Ancient records show that the people of Sumer were black. What happened to them?"

"Ah," the old man sighed. "They lost their history; so they died."[32]

Are the Sumerians dead? Well, not completely. They will live in our memory. At least for us, their black identity will not be hidden, ignored, or explained away. They have modern kinfolk who are proud of their achievements. Welcome back, Sumerian brothers. You once were lost, but now you're found.

The ancient Sumerians would be shocked to know that in this era some are trying to label their kinfolk "intellectually inferior." Modern books like *The Bell Curve* carry this as part of their message. They should put this little truth on their bell curve. The black Sumerians had "superior intellectual qualities," according to R. K. Harrison. Not only that, but they, too, have a legacy of founding civilizations.

Along with Egypt and Ethiopia in Africa, the Sumerians were the first to achieve intellectual greatness. All of mankind is indebted to these great people for the knowledge they discovered and passed on to the rest of mankind.

You would have to be deaf, dumb, and blind not to notice this trend. Wherever you find the earliest and greatest achievements of mankind in building civilizations, you will find blackness. Black people—without fail—dominate the area. These achievements occurred on their soil, where they lived. Not in Europe, where the white folk lived. The evidence is so obvious, nothing but racism could explain why these truths aren't well known.[33]

Many intellectuals in Western civilization have been hiding behind a wall of arrogance, deception, and unspeakable sin. They have stopped at almost nothing to escape the truth that the Negro founded human civilization. They go so far it even gets funny sometimes. You may find yourself having a good belly laugh listening to some of the silly stories created to steal the black man's glory and give it to Caucasians.

Scholars? They ought to be ashamed of themselves.

HOMEBOY HIGHLIGHTS, ONE MORE TIME

And you thought the homeboys had it going on only in Africa! In Mesopotamia, too, black folk accomplished feats that required advanced engineering knowledge and expertise.[34] Sumerian authority, S. N. Kramer, provides us with excellent insight into these achievements: the Sumerians built complex systems of "canals, dikes, weirs (dams), and reservoirs." They developed surveys and plans that required the use of "leveling instruments, measuring rods, drawings, and mapping." They also built great schools of learning. In these schools, evidence of their mathematical genius has been found. Tables of complex numerical systems have been unearthed. Archaeologists have also discovered in their schools groupings of algebraic problems including the answers to complicated mathematical equations. How's that for dedication to education? The Sumerians were also engaged in elaborate "chemical operations and procedures."[35]

Along with their African brothers, they were one of the first people to create writing. Their system of writing is called cuneiform by scholars.[36] In addition, these black folk were "law givers and social reformers."[37] This is nicely illustrated by the fact that a Sumerian document contains the first appearance of the word "freedom."[38]

In fact, 20th century America could learn a lesson or two about civility from this early black civilization. One of their great kings, of the Legast Dynasty, "set limits on the powers of a greedy bureaucracy, reduced taxes, put a stop to injustice, and took special pains to help the poor, widows, and the orphans."[39]

Have you noticed the decay of morals, ethics, and the increase in violence in our country? And how about the loss of honesty as a prized virtue?

The Sumerians had the good sense to prize virtues important to maintaining high standards in society. Summarizing this Sumerian quality, Kramer observes, "According to their own records, they cherished goodness and truth, law and order, justice and freedom, righteousness and straightforwardness, mercy and compassion. And they abhorred evil and falsehood, lawlessness and disorder, injustice and oppression, sinfulness and perversity, cruelty and pitilessness."[40]

Black brothers, this is your heritage. These are the values your ancestors cherished and what made them great. Know your history. Learn from the achievements of your ancestors. But not only that, learn from their mistakes also. There are plenty of those to go around for all mankind. As the Scriptures say, "All have sinned and come short of the glory of God" (Romans 3:23). Remember Nimrod? He was great without question. But he made a serious mistake. Let's talk about it.

PRIDE COMES BEFORE THE FALL

Nimrod not only built great cities in the land of Shinar (Gen. 10:11), he also went into Assyria and built the great city of Nineveh and other cities: Rehoboth, Ir, Calah, and Resen—also called the great city (Gen.

10:12). Since Nimrod was black, does that mean the original Syrians were black? Good question! What's the answer? You know me by now; get me an eyewitness!

Let me introduce Strabo, a Greek geographer born about 63 B.C. That's right. He is an eyewitness of the biblical world.[41] He states, ". . .the Syrians were black. . . ."[42] In fact, many of the original peoples inhabiting these areas were considered by the ancients to be Negroes.[43] The Chaldeans and Phoenicians were all originally recognized as black folk.[44]

The Bible tells us that Nimrod founded the city of Babel. At that time, man was speaking only one language. The people said, in their pride, with Nimrod as the leader, "Come, let us build for us a city, and a tower whose top will reach into heaven, and let us make for ourselves a name; lest we be scattered abroad over the face of the whole earth" (Gen. 11:4).

Here we find the people wanting to make a name for themselves. To be glorious and mighty. They also wanted to stay together, united by their one common language. It is interesting to note that the black Sumerians retained in their records ideas that sound nearly identical to this biblical account.

Scholars have discovered in several essays that the Sumerians had an intense hunger for glory and renown.[45] These black people considered themselves, their writings reveal, a special community "in more intimate contact with the gods than the rest of mankind."[46] By the way, you will recall that the ancients also put the Ethiopians in this lofty spiritual position.

However, as scholars point out, this belief did not result in an arrogant disregard for humanity. As we saw earlier, they were very humanitarian. Now catch this. These black folk retained a "vision of all mankind living in peace and security."[47] The Sumerians envisioned man living in harmony, held together by a common language.[48] This vision they had, however, wasn't about the future. It was a cherished memory of a time long, long ago.[49] I ask you. Does this not sound like the biblical account of the people's thoughts in Genesis 11:4 and God's response in Genesis 10:5-9? The vision side of this thing sounds wonderful. So what was wrong?

The problem was pride. It represented open rebellion against God.

Independence from Him is the root cause of all sin. God had commanded man to expand and populate the entire earth (Gen. 9:1).

Allen P. Gross in his insights on Genesis 11 in *The Bible Knowledge Commentary* explains the situation well. He points out that their desire "to enhance their unity and strength" had great potential for evil. That's why God said, "If . . . they have begun to do this, then nothing they plan to do will be impossible for them." God demonstrates His supreme power in immediate judgment. As noted above, unity was the one quality prized by the people as the secret to their strength. God quickly destroyed their unity. How? By confounding their language.[50]

Dr. Gross goes on to say that "what they considered their greatest fear—scattering—came naturally on them." The Lord scattered them all over the earth. Since then, multiple dialects, divisions, and scattering have plagued all mankind.[51]

However, black scholar Chancellor Williams points out something interesting in his book *The Destruction of Black Civilization*. Egypt periodically suffered from the problems stated above. Petty competitions between leaders, disunity, the eventual scattering from the Nile Valley into all Africa, and separation resulting in numerous dialects were the special features that stand out as the cause of black decline.[52] He claims that the struggle for preeminence among black leaders and difficulties in uniting plague the black man in America even to this day.

GOD RESISTS THE PROUD

Again, what was Nimrod's error? He thought he was so "bad" he didn't need God anymore. A fatal mistake. A monstrous sin. The wages of sin is always death (Romans 6:23). God will always humble those who lift themselves up in pride.[53] Scattering, Dr. Ross says, even with its wars is better for man than unified rebellion against God. If man would not fulfill God's mandate to fill the earth and subdue it, he would accomplish it through God's judgment.[54] God's will shall be performed even in the face of man's rebellion.[55]

Thankfully, God plans a reversal of what happened at the Tower of Babel. It will happen through the personal return of Jesus Christ in His millennial kingdom. In Jesus' kingdom, men will speak one language and worship God in glorious harmony.[56]

After God confounded the languages at Babel, mankind spread over the known world. With God's encouragement, they began to fulfill His command to populate and subdue the earth (Gen. 1:28).

I can understand populate, but how would they subdue it? They were to subdue the earth by studying it and using the knowledge gained to benefit creation.[57] This should be the real purpose behind all science and technology.[58] The black man, in particular, after the scattering, led the way in this regard. The genius and creativity placed in the Hamites did not leave them when they journeyed to Arabia and Africa.

You know why? They were too legit to quit! The black man would create civilization again in Ethiopia and her oldest daughter Egypt. This time it would be in Africa, which became their primary homeland, where their earthly splendor and glory would continue.

The biblical, archeological, anthropological, and eyewitness evidence come together to state this undeniable truth. All of the descendants of Ham "meet the American definition of a Negro."[59] It should be clear by now that the black man is the fountain, the very spring, out of which civilization as we know it has flowed.

We've covered a lot of ground, haven't we? Thank you for your patience. I have only one final observation to make in concluding this chapter. Y'all were "terrible from the beginning!"

Time Out

1. Describe the method for finding blacks in the Bible.

2. Identify one thing you can do now to regain your history for yourself, your children, and your people.

3. What are two lessons you can learn from the account of Nimrod and the Tower of Babel (Genesis 11)? How can this be applied to your personal return to glory?

TIME OUT (CONT.)

4. If you are not of African descent, can you imagine yourself leading a class on the information shared in this chapter? Why or why not?

7 | Lord, Don't You Care?

The black man. Famous; enormously successful; and too legit to quit. He did it all without singing and dancing or playing football, basketball, or baseball. Standing out with brain as well as brawn. You have to hand it to him. His past was glorious. Through our study of the Table of Nations in Genesis 10, we put meat on the bones of Isaiah's impressive description of the Ethiopian. However, we're going to soon find out that Isaiah 18's message for the black man involved more than past glories. It also had something vital to say about his future. To receive that message from God, we must turn our attention back to Isaiah 18.

OH, HOW THE MIGHTY HAVE FALLEN

Let's pick up Isaiah's message in Isaiah 18:3. It reads, "All inhabitants of the world and dwellers on the earth: when He lifts up a banner on the mountains you see it, and when He blows a trumpet, you hear it." Hold up. What's the trumpet symbol all about? God is sounding the alarm to get people's attention. He wants the entire world "to take notice of what He is about to do."[1] The trumpet actually is a proclamation of war.[2] He is about to accomplish a mighty work which calls for Him to enter the scene as the "Lord of Hosts" (verse 7).[3]

By the way, "Lord of Hosts" is God's military name. Later we will explain the significance of this name in understanding the meaning of this chapter. For now I'll leave you with this thought. When God's ready to bang like a warrior . . . ready to take matters into His own hands. When He is of a mind to say to the devil, *Make my day,* this is the name He uses.[4] Something awesome is going down when God calls Himself the "Lord of Hosts."

For the moment, let's move on to verse 4. It reads, "For so the Lord said to me, 'I will take my rest, and I will look from My dwelling place like clear heat in sunshine, like a cloud of dew in the heat of harvest.'" This looks like God is "cooling out," as some say. Resting. What does this mean? The verse is telling us that before God goes to battle, just prior to His cleaning house, He is going to appear as an unconcerned spectator.[5] He's going to be looking from His dwelling place quietly. Exactly what is it that He looks unconcerned about? Good question. Are you ready for the answer? He is going to look unconcerned about the fall and humiliation of the black man.

Let me back up a second. Please bear with me, because a lot of folk have stumbled over these verses. I want to describe for you the context of this passage. It will aid our understanding. Better dust off your dancing shoes again. You're going to need them.

FITTING THE PATTERN

This Isaiah 18 passage is part of a section of Isaiah that deals with pronouncements of judgments on nations. The section begins with chapter 13 and ends with chapter 23.[6] In each pronouncement, a specific nation is identified and warned. The nature of their judgment is then described with varying degrees of detail.

This seems very simple, so why am I taking the time to explain it? The reason is this. Some commentators have violated the context and have taken the prophecy against Ethiopia and applied it to Assyria.[7] In other words, they have made it seem as though, at first, God is warning the Cushites about impending judgment. Then, strangely enough, He turns and describes a judgment on the Assyrians. The fact that He had already pronounced judgment against Assyria in the prior chapter makes it even more strange.

This is very confusing and makes the phrase "Woe to the land shadowed with buzzing wings" very unnecessary. The confusion is aggravated further by some commentators' translation of "scattered and peeled" in Isaiah 18:2. We talked about this in the chapter "They Can Dance, Too." This "scattered and peeled" phrase takes on more importance if the judgments in verses 5 and 6 apply to Assyria. Why? There has to be something negative for the Cushites in this passage to justify the "woe" they were given at the start. The judgment pronounced in verses 5 and 6 is clearly directed against the Cushites.

That's enough time on the confusion. Let's turn ourselves again to the real meaning of the passage.

THE BLACK MAN'S FALL FROM GLORY

The 25th Dynasty. We already pointed out that the black brothers of this Dynasty were in charge of Egypt at the time of this prophecy. Chancellor Williams, a black scholar, observes that this Dynasty has "special significance for the black world." The reason for this is not that the Dynasty was created by black folk.[8] But because the conclusion of their reign, 730-656 B.C. brings to an end black efforts to retake control of Egyptian civilization.[9] By 661 B.C., Assyrian forces pushed African armies south of northern Egypt.[10] This defeat marked the beginning point of black decline in the world.[11]

This is not to say there were no further glories. But black civilization would not have the world dominance that it once enjoyed. History records all too vividly the tremendous fall of the black man. He occupied the highest pinnacle of human greatness. Renowned, respected, and at times even worshipped. Now, at the bottom of humanity, relegated to an inferior status all over the world.[12]

It could not be otherwise. For this was the judgment prophesied in Isaiah 18. Yet, we were not alone. Other nations received God's judgment. Babylon, Philistia, Moab, Assyria, Edom, Arabia, Tyre, and Israel were all judged and fell. "But the horrors of our judgment seem so great!" you say. You're right. And this is just. "For to whom much is given, much will be required" (Luke 12:48). This is a divine principle. God applies it without partiality.

Consider the Jews. As God's chosen people, they were given great blessings and opportunities. Through them came the Scriptures, the Word of the living God. They enjoyed a special covenant relationship with the Almighty. They were given much, so much was required. When they periodically fell into unbelief and rebellion, they were defeated by heathen nations and at times made into slaves.

Finally, through continuous rebellion, they were scattered all over the world. Often hated and persecuted, they were without a homeland from 70 A.D. until 1948. We need not review here the despicable horrors of Nazi Germany and its impact on the Jews in the 20th century. These cruelties are well known.

Take notice. It is no coincidence that blacks and Jews together have this trait in common. They are the most renown examples of extreme persecution on this planet. God has used heathen nations, more sinful than His people, to discipline his people. This brought complaints from God's prophets. Eventually, he will judge all ungodly nations including those that were used to discipline His own.

The New Testament book of James states the principle of responsibility in another way. Teachers are warned, "My brethren, let not many of you become teachers, knowing that we shall receive a stricter judgment" (James 3:1).

THE AFRICAN-JEWISH CONNECTION

Renowned Bible teacher, Dr. Tony Evans, observes that there is a strong Jewish and African link in the Bible. They lived together and interacted throughout their respective histories. Early on, especially, much inter-breeding occurred. For example, the Jewish tribes of Manasseh and Ephraim were the offspring of Joseph's marriage to an Egyptian woman (Genesis 41:50-52). Moses' father-in-law, Jethro, was a black man.[13] He was the father of the Ethiopian woman Moses married, referred to in Numbers 12. Phinehas was a priest in the commonwealth of Israel. Guess what Phinehas means in Hebrew? It means "the Negro" or "the Nubian" (Exodus 6:25; 1 Chronicles 9:20).[14] This black man from the Aaronic priestly line also led military forces under Moses.

The Original African Heritage Bible contains an interesting 19th century article. In it there is a section showing how Africa was often a place of refuge for the Hebrew people. The writer started with Abraham and ended with Jesus to make his point. Here is a summary. Abraham, when famine struck, was preserved from death in Africa. Jacob and his sons similarly were preserved from death in Africa. Moses, "the greatest law giver the world has ever known, was born and educated" in Africa. Jesus, as a young child, "was preserved from death." Where? In Africa. When the Son of God was struggling up to Calvary, barely able to carry the cross, "accused by Asia, condemned by Europe," it was Africa that delivered the man (Simon of Cyrene) to help Him with His burden.[15]

CAN'T YOU SEE MY PAIN?

I have at times questioned God about the plight of the black man. I don't know about you, but I wondered how He could allow our people to experience the humiliation of American racism. A humiliation that continues in some form even today. Sometimes I'd say, "God don't you care about this situation." It has appeared at times that He wasn't that concerned about it. This was an especially bothersome issue in light of the indifference of so-called Christian churches.

The perception that racism is low on God's agenda is exactly what God predicted in Isaiah 18:4-5. "Yes it may seem that way for a time. Like I'm resting, unconcerned, looking from my dwelling place."

Brothers, let me tell you something. God is more than concerned about racism. He is downright angry about it. If America thinks it can coddle this sin, it better think again. The first warning God gave was called the Civil War. Many Christians, both white and black, believe that war was God's judgment on this country. Why? For refusing to heed His repeated warnings to abolish the evil of slavery. Over 600,000 men were killed. That's more American deaths suffered than WW I, WW II, and Vietnam combined.[16]

JUDGMENT BEGINS AT HOME

There is a mighty move of the Spirit happening in the church in America. A central element of this move of God is a head on confrontation with the sin of racism. Like never before, men and women are being moved to deal with this horrible sin. Racial reconciliation, for the obedient ones, is a major concern of the heart. The Lord of Hosts is resting no more. The banner is raised, the trumpet is blown.

Brothers, God is preparing a great work of deliverance and healing for the black man. It will astound the world and it will glorify Jesus. Glorify Jesus? That's right. God has fixed it, so He gets the glory.

Are you ready now for God's message about your future? It's time to bring it home now. We're going to conclude our study of Isaiah 18 by expounding the last 3 verses of the chapter. Open your heart. It would be hard to overemphasize the importance of what you're going to read next.

Time Out

1. Have you ever wondered if God really cares about racism? Or about you?

2. Did you ever feel as though God loved you and your people less than others? Did this affect your relationship with God? How? Did this affect your relationship with others? How?

3. What has this chapter taught you about God's view of the African American?

4. If you are not of African descent, have you ever examined your heart concerning racial prejudice? Why or why not? How will this chapter change your view of this issue (sin)? What will you do about it?

8 | Down, But Not Out

Truth. A rare commodity today. Honesty is even more difficult to find. I'd rather someone give it to me straight. No sugar coating and "no slippin' and slidin', peepin' and hidin'," as my dad used to say. For me, it's about respect. Because I respect you, I'm going to deal with you straight up. That's our style in teaching the Bible. When the Word makes us look good, I love it. When it makes us look bad . . . well, I don't like it as much. But I know God's truth is good for me. So I accept it.

WHAT TIME IS IT?

Do you still have your Bible? Turn back to Isaiah 18:5. This verse opens up with three very important words: "Before the harvest. . . ." These three words are placing a time element on the fulfillment of the prophecy.[1] The Bible is making it clear that black people will experience all that follows "before the harvest." When is that?

The answer to the question is found in Matthew 13:39.[2] Jesus, in that verse, defines "the harvest" as meaning the end of the age. Now that we know the meaning of "harvest," we can accurately interpret Isaiah 18:5. The passage is teaching that before Jesus returns to earth to establish His kingdom all these things will be fulfilled.

WORKING IN THE GARDEN

Let's finish reading verse 5. "For before the harvest, when the bud is perfect and the sour grape is ripening in the flower, He will both cut off the sprigs with pruning hooks and take away and cut down the branches." Pretty strong isn't it? God is saying in this verse that He will cut down the black man's glory. When? Like with grapes, just when they're beginning to ripen. This is a reference to the Nubian/Ethiopian dynasty and its recent rise to fame. We made this point earlier. But it deserves to be restated. The idea of black folk repeating the feat of the first black pharaoh 2300 years earlier seemed impossible.[3]

Remember chapter 3. The first Pharaoh, known by the Greeks as Menes, was the homeboy who first united all of Egypt in 3200 B.C. He expanded Ethiopia's power northward to the shores of the Mediterranean.[4] But by this time, the Asians were so powerful in Egypt, the brothers from the south didn't seem able to subdue them.[5] When Piankhi and his Ethiopian generals succeeded in pushing the Asians out and re-established control of northern Egypt, the people were overjoyed.[6] The Egyptians shouted, "The rightful rulers of our land have returned!"[7]

The 25th Dynasty, once their power was consolidated, started a "powerful movement of cultural and . . . national" revival.[8] This included the restoration of Egyptian monuments and a revival of their ancient religion.[9] It didn't last long, however. Not even a hundred years.

In 661 B.C. Assyria attacked Egypt and destroyed its most ancient and glorious city, the city of Thebes.[10] This date, as mentioned before, "marked the decline of black . . . supremacy" in world history.[11]

The fall of the 25th Dynasty was tragic. What looked like the beginning of a new era of power was quickly over. The Divine Gardener had begun His work.

LOOKING UP AT BOTTOM

When you want to destroy a tree what do you do—cut the root, or cut the branches? Naturally, you cut the root. God isn't messing with the root here. He is pruning branches. In fact, pruning branches is something you do to help a plant bear even more fruit. Keep that thought in the back of your mind. It will serve us well later. Let's move on.

The cutting of the branches, in part, refers to the African slave trade.[12] We won't spend the time detailing the horrors of that evil trafficking in human lives. But it wouldn't hurt to recall its devastation. One French historian notes that it would be "no exaggeration" to say that Africa lost 100 million people.[13] Dr. W. E. B. DuBois, the great African American historian, agrees with the figures.[14]

We must remember, African slaves were sent not only to America, but also to Europe, the West Indies, and to Persia in the East.[15] Slave wars took the lives of many. Others succumbed to illness and injury.[16] Still others "were cast adrift to die of hunger and starvation."[17] In 1871, several years after the American Civil War, David Livingston said, "It is awful, but I cannot speak of the slaving for fear of appearing guilty of exaggerating."[18]

From a people having near infinite power (Nahum 3:9) to a bloody victimization in the African slave trade. How did it happen? Let's break it down to the lowest common denominator. Our people were so great, they got beside themselves. When you think you're so bad that you don't need God anymore, trouble is coming. God's response? I'll give it to you in one sentence: "I'll have to humble you, so I can use you."[19]

MERCY IN JUDGMENT

While black civilization declined politically, God already had plans to move spiritually. Few people know that the first and oldest Christian nation is black: the country of Ethiopia. Furthermore, by the 6th century, Nubia, a black African country south of Upper Egypt, was entirely Christianized.[20] These great people, whose ancestors were kings of the 25th Dynasty, gave their hearts to Jesus. Historians reveal that, "During the Christian period, the Nubians were highly regarded."[21] The people inhabiting the Near East knew them "for their great beauty and high moral virtues."[22]

In the end, their faith in Jesus cost them their civilization.[23] The Muslims, determined to destroy Christianity in Nubia, sought to do it by force. It would take a lot more than threats and speeches to get those brothers to bow to Allah. In fact, it took the Muslims no less than five military expeditions to finally succeed.[24] Such was the Nubian brothers' commitment to Christ, it took "1,000 years of bloody persecution" to remove the Nubian church.[25]

The Muslims, through use of force and other means, succeeded in spreading their religion throughout Africa.[26] Don't forget this fact, however. The black man embraced Christianity hundreds of years before Islam even existed. It was Africa that first sent Christian missionaries to Europe, not Europe to Africa. Some of the church's first great theologians came from Africa. Ever hear of St. Augustine and Tertullian? Africans, my brother.

It wasn't until the mid 1300s that Muslims succeeded in pushing their dominance and control south of Egypt.[27] This was an unfortunate development for the black man. For when it came to targeting blacks only for slaves, Muslims were first.[28] What a lot of people don't know is that the Muslims raided, raped, and enslaved Africans as ruthlessly as the Europeans did. Know Your History.

The Islamic religion was Satan's plan for "snuffing out" the Word of God.[29] For if African people converted to Islam, God would be left with no true worshipers "beyond the rivers of Ethiopia."[30] Then how would the prophecy of Zephaniah 3:10 be fulfilled?

Sure enough, many of our people eventually converted to Islam. But God had an answer to that devilish strategy. He permitted a slave trade.[31] But something special happened in the process of preparing us by humbling us: "God touched the heart of the white slave master."[32] What man meant for evil, God would turn to good. Let's talk about it.

A WELCOMED RE-INTRODUCTION

What do you mean? How did God open the heart of the white slavemaster? He did it in this way. The white Christian slave master began teaching the slaves about Jesus.[33] He told them that Jesus loved them, that Jesus had died for their sins—and if they believed, they would have eternal life. The black man received the message, by and large, with an open heart.

This amazes me. Even though the messenger was his oppressor, the black man saw past the evil and beheld the glory of God. Awesome, isn't it? The message of our God and Savior Jesus Christ was so beautiful, even the white man couldn't mess it up. Yet we were not getting something new. We weren't introduced to Jesus. We were RE-introduced to Him.[34]

In the midst of our tremendous suffering, we heard there was a God who cares. We began to sing "We are climbing Jacob's ladder!" in our praises to God.[35] At times, to be honest, when we sang that song . . . well, what we really meant was, "We're getting out of here tonight!"[36]

TURNED ON TO GOD

It worked. Our people got on fire for the Lord. God had brought us from Africa to re-introduce us to Jesus. Remember Zephaniah 3:10? Let me quote it for you again: "From beyond the rivers of Ethiopia, my worshipers will bring an offering to me." It was like God was saying, "Yes, you are my worshipers. Time to come home." You couldn't keep those slaves from praising Jesus. "For the slave, the worship service was the only time he was free," explains Dr. Tony Evans.[37] It was a celebration of God.[38]

Have you noticed something, brothers? I know you have if you've been in enough black churches. Celebrating God in worship is still happening.[39] Shouting, dancing, singing, and praising are distinctive features of most black worship in America.[40] This is biblical. Read Psalm 92. When our folk "go from shouting, to dancing, to praising and crying," they are in line with the Word of God.[41]

Even white folks started worshipping like this recently.[42] They got involved in what is being called the "charismatic movement." Some of these white Christians are louder than we are now.[43] But we didn't need any "movement" to free us up to express with emotion our admiration for God. It's part of who we are when we accept Him. Why? God foretold that we would be His worshipers. It's in our hearts, souls, and spirits to exalt the Lord with exuberant praise.

Those precious black saints. Slaves in a foreign land. Yes, you could hear them singing as they worked tirelessly in the fields. Under the burden of back breaking labor, you could hear joyful voices ringing through the air. "Swing low sweet chariot, coming for to carry me home. . . ." Oppression couldn't stop them. Hunger couldn't stop them. Hatred couldn't stop them. The master's whip couldn't stop them. Nothing could keep our people from praising His holy name. You're right Lord. We are Your worshipers.

BACK TO THE FUTURE

Slavery. A part of our past, but not the end of the story. We're going to bring this message through to the 20th century and down to this very hour. The next chapter will conclude our study of Isaiah 18. As you will soon see, we were down, but not out. God had planned from the beginning that you black brothers would rise again. Look up, for your "Return to Glory" draws near.

Time Out

1. In what way(s) are your parents like God in "pruning" the sprigs and branches in your life?

2. How have you been re-introduced to Jesus?

3. Read John 3:16 and Romans 10:9, 10 from the Bible. What must a person do to be saved?

4. Does this chapter bring you hope and encouragement about your future? If so, why?

5. What information shared in this chapter demonstrates God's deep love for black people?

6. If you are not of African descent, how did this chapter affect your view of black people? In what ways will it change you? Why?

9 | Come Out With Your Hands Up

The African American male. A descendant of "a long line of giants, unsurpassed by any people on earth!"[1] Sadly, his present condition doesn't reflect this fact. One author calls him an "endangered species." The statistics are gruesome. The massive homicides in the inner city are staggering. We have high teenage pregnancy rates, with black fathers nowhere to be found. 50 percent of the prison population is black, while only 12 percent of the total population is black.[2] Drug addiction is also widespread.

SATAN'S FIELD DAY

Isaiah 18:6 is a prophecy foretelling the development of facts referenced above. It reads, "They will be left together for the mountain birds of prey and for the beasts of the earth; the birds of prey will summer on them, and all the beasts of the earth will winter on them."

There are several symbols here. I'll define their probable meanings so we can better understand the text. "Birds of prey" is a reference to Satan.[3] Just before the harvest, Satan is going to have a "field day" on black folk.[4] Again, this is evidenced by the conditions in the black community mentioned above.

The term "beasts of the earth" is often a reference to men.[5] In fact the man who will be the last great dictator of the world is called "the beast." (See Revelation 13:4.) The term "wintering" means to bring reproach[6] on a person, which means to discredit or disgrace someone.[7]

Putting the terms together we have the following interpretation: Satan will be the main instigator of the deception and oppression of many black people. A major part of this judgment will be men bringing a reproach on black people all over the world. How did they do?

Quite well. Europe and America get the gold medal. They have been predominantly responsible for the distorted image of black folks across this world. In many cases, black has come to mean inferior. This is the result of one of the most systematic, persistent campaigns in history. The educational system, the political system, the economic system, the social system, the media, and popular cultural myths have cooperated in promoting this agenda.

The year 1800 saw the escalation of this war on the black soul.[8] What happened? Napoleon's army had recently opened up Egypt for European archeologist and historians.[9] American scholars would soon follow. As they studied, translated Egyptian documents, and unearthed monuments, one very disturbing truth emerged.[10] Black Africa, it was clear, was the mother of all civilization.[11] They were beside themselves. That unwelcomed discovery generated the most massive disinformation campaign in history.[12]

These revelations couldn't have come at a worse time. Europe was in power and enslaving black people. Not to mention profiting handsomely from the enterprise. Simultaneously, white Christians against slavery and other abolitionists were proclaiming with increasing vigor the evil of this perverse institution.

So what was the purpose of rewriting history? To debase the Negro "at any cost and in all minds."[13] Priority number one was to "destroy the memory of a Negro Egypt."[14] Most people today are ignorant of this fact. Before 1800, it was a commonly accepted truth in academic environments that ancient Egypt had been a "Negro" civilization.[15]

Thankfully, God always preserves a remnant of people who keep their integrity. But many didn't. When the denial of a black Egypt began, scholars were fully aware that they were running a scam.

Great white scholars like Count Constantine de Volney were thorns in the side for racists. For example, Champollion-Figeac, a prejudiced French Egyptologist, was beside himself because "the Count" was well read and had his books in most libraries.[16]

We quoted Count de Volney before, but it seems appropriate to do it again. After visiting Egypt he wrote, "The ancient Egyptians were true Negroes of the same type as all native born Africans. . . . Just think that this race of black men, today our slave and object of our scorn, is the very race to which we owe our arts, sciences, and even the use of speech."[17]

The above quote is a good, concise summary of Isaiah 18:1-6. It could not be explained any better.

THE PARTY IS OVER

There comes a time when God's patience runs out. He's long-suffering to be sure, but it isn't endless. This is especially true when people He loves are being "dogged" by their enemies.

Remember, God heard the cries of the Jews under bondage in Egypt. In His time, He decided to act. He sent Moses to tell old Pharaoh, "Let my people go." Pharaoh resisted. God Himself fought the battle for His people's freedom, taking no prisoners along the way. Pharaoh had no choice but to let God's people go.

A "let my people go" kind of message is heralding from the throne of God today. The spiritually sensitive are hearing it. Satan has been put on notice and is upset about it. The devil knows his ugly party is coming to a close.

In the midst of the black man's degradation, while Satan is having a field day, "The Lord of Hosts" is going to do something dramatic. That conforms to God's style. He likes to enter into situations that look hopeless from man's point of view. Then by His own hand, He accomplishes the impossible.

It's like when Moses and the children of Israel were trapped during the Exodus. In front of them was the Red Sea, and behind them was the most advanced army on earth. The whole camp was terrified. Men and women were screaming, and the animals were stampeding.[18]

In the midst of the chaos, Moses stood up and shouted, "Do not be afraid. Stand still, and see the salvation of the Lord, which He will accomplish for you today. For the Egyptians whom you see today, you shall see again no more forever. The Lord will fight for you, and you shall hold your peace" (Exodus 14:13).

The Exodus is one of the most well-known stories in biblical history. The deliverance God performed involved the splitting of the Red Sea. The Jews passed through on dry ground. The Egyptian army in pursuit was drowned every one. This is the God we're dealing with in Isaiah 18:7. The "Lord of Hosts" is back!

Let's read. "In that time a present will be brought to the Lord of

Hosts from a people tall and smooth of skin, and from a people terrible from their beginning onward, a nation powerful and treading down, whose land the rivers divide, to the place of the Lord of Hosts, to Mount Zion" (Isaiah 18:7).

This is really unique. It stands out all the more because this section of Isaiah is dealing with judgments on the nations. You see, God is declaring, along with the judgment, a marvelous promise concerning the future of black people. He intends for nobody to be confused about this.

God has a good reason for anticipating misunderstanding. The potential for confusion exists because of the terrible fall that these folks will experience. They will be in such a low estate as a result of this judgment people could easily conclude a promising future could never happen.

Can you see what God is doing here to make sure you don't miss it? Well, let me say it this way. He could have simply stated the Ethiopian will bring Him a present. But instead He repeats the rather lengthy description He gives of these people in verses 1 and 2. Why? God wants it real plain. In fact, unmistakably clear. For those very same people who received the judgment have been promised a mighty deliverance and blessing before the end of the age.

THE NAME THAT BINDS

We mentioned earlier the importance of names in the Bible. This is even more important with the names of God. When God identifies Himself by a particular name, it is essential that you check it out. Some of this we have already done in our study. We identified the name, The "Lord of Hosts," which God uses in this passage as God's military name. He uses this name when He considers the battle His—when He will guarantee victory with His own might.

Listen carefully. We're getting ready to see an example of the beautiful harmony of the Word of God. Although the "Lord of Hosts" is God's military name, it doesn't involve typical military style behavior from His people. Dr. Herbert Lockyer, in his book, *All the Divine Names and Titles in the Bible,* makes this instructive observation. "In the great majority of passages where the title (the Lord of Hosts) is found, there is no allusion to war. . . . The title seems to point to the relation of God to His people when gathered together for service and worship." This is important. God uses this title when gathering His people for worship.

In Isaiah 18:7, in His promise concerning black people, God selects the name that signals the gathering of His worshipers. Remember what God called His black children in Zephaniah 3:10? He called them "My worshipers."

It is now time to bring to the table the prophecy concerning black people in Psalm 68:31. It reads, "Ethiopia will quickly stretch out her hands to God." This, my brothers, is an act of WORSHIP. The Living Bible translates the same verse, "Ethiopia will stretch out her hands to God in adoration."

The circle is now complete. Isaiah 18:7, Zephaniah 3:10, and Psalm 68:31 come together in beautiful harmony. God selects the name that He uses when gathering His worshipers (Zephaniah 3:10) together. They will at that time stretch out their hands in adoration and praise to Him (Psalm 68:31).

That His people are "beyond" the rivers of Ethiopia is significant. How far beyond? Even to the shores of America. The place where black slaves, re-introduced to Jesus, embraced Him once again. As they respond to His message of grace, like no other people, they will distinctively praise and worship the Lord just as God foretold they would. It is no coincidence that right after black folk "stretch out their hands" in praise, the Bible exhorts, "Sing to God, you kingdoms of the earth; oh, sing praises to the Lord" (Psalm 68:32 NKJV).

UNWRAPPING THE PRESENT

What is this present that black folk will bring to the Lord? Let's see if we can find some clues in the Word. Zephaniah 3:10 is as good a place to start the search as any. It says, "The daughter of My dispersed ones shall bring My offering." This verse indicates the present will be an offering of some kind. Another word for offering would be sacrifice.

Psalm 68:31 informs us that the Ethiopian will stretch forth his hands in adoration of the Lord. As we pointed out earlier, this is an act of worship. Psalm 68:30, just prior to this prophecy, gives us another important clue. It reads, "Envoys will come out of Egypt." The Living Bible paraphrase explains the verse this way, "Egypt will send gifts of precious metals."

There is a contrast here. Egypt brings a material, physical, tangible gift. Ethiopia's gift is not physical or material like that of Egypt. It is a spiritual gift of humble adoration and praise.

A SACRIFICE OF PRAISE

Is there such a thing as an offering or sacrifice of praise? There certainly is. The Bible talks about it in Hebrews 13:15. It reads, "Therefore, by Him then, let us continually offer the sacrifice of praise to God, That is, the fruit of our lips giving thanks to His name."

God is well pleased with such sacrifices (Hebrews 13:16). Praise, then, is an offering (sacrifice), a gift if you will, that God is delighted to receive. But let me assure you of this. God is not speaking simply of your lips forming words of praise. It must be sincere and from the heart.

When Jesus was on earth He denounced some of the Jewish leaders (especially the Pharisees) as hypocrites. His charge against them? "This people draws near to Me with their mouths, and honor me with their lips, but their heart is far from Me" (Matthew 15:8). Your "sacrifice of praise" is only as good as the sincerity of your heart.

In order for your words of praise to be an acceptable offering, you yourself must be an offering. Your life, too, must be a sacrifice to God. The Apostle Paul teaches this in Romans 12:1 where he says to believers, "I urge you, therefore, brethren, by the mercies of God, To present your bodies a living and holy sacrifice, acceptable to God, which is your spiritual service of worship" (Romans 12:1 NASB).

This is critical. Paul is saying believers should devote their lives to God as a "holy sacrifice." When you as a people are a sacrifice, then your "sacrifice of praise" is a delightful present unto the Lord.

This leads me to an interesting observation. Turn with me again to Isaiah 18:7. The Hebrew construction of this sentence could be translated to mean THE PEOPLE THEMSELVES ARE THE PRESENT.[19]

The popular Bible commentator, Matthew Henry, explains it this way in his book entitled *The Matthew Henry Commentary*. He says, ". . .a people . . . shall be a present to the Lord . . . though they seem useless and worthless, they shall be an acceptable present to Him. . . ." In making his comments, he refers to the prophecy of Psalm 68:31 concerning the

Ethiopians. Although lacking a clear revelation in other parts of this passage, Henry did catch this important point. The people themselves are a present to the Lord. A praising and worshipping people.

FAIR WEATHER PRAISING

Black brothers, you and your people are to be a present to the Lord in this final hour. In a special way, you are uniquely positioned to be a sacrifice of praise to your God. Why? Because praising God when things have been wonderful and when you're on top of the world is not the "sacrifice of praise." Sure enough, we should praise God and give thanks when things are good. God is pleased with this. But it doesn't fit the category of praise as a sacrifice.[20]

It is when things are not going well. When you're misunderstood, persecuted, and condemned. When your circumstances are painful and the devil is on your back. Yet in spite of it all, you stand up like a man. You're a warrior. You face your circumstances and defy the devil by saying, "Lord, I praise Your name!"

When the tears of sorrow are falling down your cheek, nevertheless, unmovable you shout from your heart, "Glory to your name, Lord Jesus. I praise your name."[21] That, my brother, is the sacrifice of praise!!

ONLY ONE RESPONSE

There was a Hebrew king by the name of Jehoshaphat. He and his people were surrounded by a vast army. He didn't know what to do. Outnumbered, he feared their possible destruction. He went to inquire of the prophets as to what course of action to take.

The prophets' answer from the Lord was, "Do not fear or be dismayed because of this great multitude, for the battle is not yours, but God's" (2 Chronicles 20:15 NASB). The Lord encouraged them further, "Don't fear or be dismayed; tomorrow go out to face them, for the Lord is with you" (2 Chron. 20:17 NASB).

Guess what the military strategy was when they went to the field of battle? Send the chariots? Nope. Send archers? Nope. You give up? Okay, I'll tell you. It was send the praisers, send the singers, and send the worshipers.

When God says the battle is Mine . . . well, there is only one instruction. Gather the worshipers. As they begin to praise, as they begin to sing, God Himself destroys the enemy. He did if for Jehoshaphat. He'll do the same for you.

A HISTORY OF HANDS

"Ethiopia will quickly stretch out her hands to God" (Psalm 68:31). God refers to your hands in this prophecy. Interesting. Dr. Clarence Walker outlines black history using the typology of hands. Let me share it with you. He calls the several hundred years up to the 1800s a time of *shackled hands* due to the horrors of the slave trade. The 1800s to 1900s he calls *calloused hands*. This was due to labor performed on plantations. The 1960s to the 1970s was a time of *clinched hands*. At that time, Dr. Walker observes, black power was our cry with a clinched fist raised in the air. He refers to the 1970s to 1980s as a time of *shaking hands*. This came from widespread drug abuse.

Guess what Dr. Walker calls the 1990s? You got it. A time of *outstretched hands*. The time when the "Lord of Hosts" sends the call to His black children—His worshipers from "beyond the rivers of Ethiopia." God's Spirit is calling the black man to come back home. Return to your God, black brothers. Come out from the bondage. Come out from the pain and the anger. Come out from the crime and drug addiction. God is prepared to do a mighty work for you as the "Lord of Hosts." The battle is His. He cannot and will not be defeated.

And "come out with your hands up!"[22] In praise and adoration to the God of your ancestors, Jesus Christ, the Lord. Like powerful spiritual warriors, bring your praises loudly and unashamedly. Like a crack archer, send your arrows of praise to the true and living God. Send it not to Mohammed, not to Elijah Mohammad, not to Allah, not to Buddha, but to Jesus! Jesus! Jesus!

God's intention is not that you praise Him with your lips alone. He has some further instructions for you. Receive your marching orders from the King of kings and Lord of lords. Let's get prepared for the battle.

BLACK MAN, COME HOME

What is God saying? What does all this mean? God is saying to you African American male, "Return to Me. I love you. I humbled you in order to use you. Because of my care for you, my plan, from the beginning included your return to glory."

Return to glory? Yes. But a glory of a different kind. You taught men science, medicine, art, religion, and engineering. You gave men civilization. You used the beauty and the genius that God put in you to build up the kingdoms of this world.

But the Lord has humbled you in order to use you in these last days to build up another kingdom. The kingdom of His dear Son. This kingdom isn't temporary like the others. They will fade and be no more. But the Son's kingdom—glory to God—will last forever!

God wants to save you, sanctify you, anoint you, and raise you up.[23] Not to be a leader in building up earthly kingdoms. But this time to show men how to praise Him, how to glorify Him, and how to worship Him.

Instead of teaching men mathematics and architecture, lead the way in teaching them how to live holy, how to live victoriously, how to deliver the captives, how to lift up the poor, and how to trample the devil to the glory of His name! Shoulder to shoulder with white, yellow, and red brothers. With all of God's children, taking His message of salvation to a lost and dying world.

Black brother, don't you hear the Spirit calling? Have you sensed in your heart that this message is from God? If you have, I urge you to answer the call. STOP reading for a moment. Look up to Jesus. Ask Him to come into your life and save you. Confess your sins and turn to Him with all your heart. He'll forgive you and bless you.

When you do, you will have taken your first step down the road of destiny. The first step of the journey on your majestic "Return to Glory."

Time Out

1. Have you been affected by one or more of the statistics listed at the beginning of this chapter? If so, in what way?

2. What are some of the areas in your life that need change? What steps can you take starting today to bring about that change sooner in these areas?

3. How did you feel after reading the quote of Count De Volney after he visited Egypt?

4. God loves you. This is seen above all in His sacrifice for your sins, but also in His prophecy concerning you. How does the fact that God has planned for your "Return to Glory" impact you? What do you want to do about this plan?

5. If you are not of African descent, how does this prophecy concerning the black man impact you? Will it affect your relationship with black folk in any way? How about your relationships within your own race? Why?

10 | What's Up With the Cover-Up?

I'm impressed. No doubt about it, you have what it takes. Nine chapters later and you're still with me. I'm assuming of course that you didn't cheat and skip some chapters to get to this one. If you got here legitimately, congratulations. I thank you for your patience and your time. We consider it a privilege to communicate what we believe is God's message to black people in this generation.

This message wouldn't be complete without some explanation of the reason behind the distortion of our history. Part of that explanation should include how they did it. Just how did European and American power centers achieve this great historical fabrication.

Some of the reasons "why" have already been hinted at and at times stated outright. Others will be revealed for the first time in this chapter. We spent even less time on "how" this deception was accomplished. This chapter will devote itself, primarily, to answering these questions.

One word of caution is in order. There is no way we can cover this subject in detail with one chapter. It would be difficult to do it in a whole book. Black professor, Martin Bernal, spends all of four volumes dismantling this masterful cover-up. For further study see professor Bernal's award winning work entitled *Black Athena*.

What we will do is give you the highlights. An overview sufficient enough to provide a basic understanding of why and how the scam was put over. Are you ready? Let's do it.

LIVING WITH A BAD CONSCIENCE

Ever do something you knew was wrong? I have. If you've "been there and done that," then you know what a guilty conscience feels like. Very unpleasant. Your first impulse is to do something to appease it or to push it into the background.

We have just touched on one of the reasons for the cover-up. Modern Egyptology (the study of Egypt) got underway at the very time when white men were enslaving black folk. Feeling guilty, white academia was busier than a one-armed paper hanger, looking for a justification for slavery.[1] Why? Again, a guilty conscience.

The slave trade was concerned about only one issue. Money! If a slave could bring no money, he was thrown overboard like a "horse with a broken leg."[2] I won't review again the devastation of the trade. I gave you a short overview of the carnage in an earlier chapter. You would think, given the situation, that human beings would have been pricked in their conscience for this cruelty to their fellow man. Many were.

In America, as early as the 1600s, some people were beginning to admit that slavery was morally wrong. In their book, *Black Cargoes,* authors Daniel P. Mannix and Malcolm Cowley document the phenomenon. They point out that Massachusetts in 1641 enacted a law called "Body of Liberties." The law stated that only prisoners of war, or strangers willingly sold, could be slaves. Another example: Rhode Island in 1652 passed a law that freed a slave after ten years, or at the age of 24 if made a slave when he was a child.[3]

The authors also highlight some important individuals. Let's look at a few. The first noteworthy American in the war against slavery was Anthony Benezet, a Quaker. He was sitting in a Quaker meeting in 1772 when the discussion turned to slavery. According to the authors, the other people discussed the issue as calmly as trading cattle. Benezet could no longer stand the inhumanity displayed in the discourse.[4]

Remember the prophecy we studied concerning the black man in Psalm 68:31? Benezet quoted it at the meeting. With his face wet with tears, he cried "Ethiopia shall soon stretch out her hands unto God!" His appeal was filled with such passion, they voted unanimously to condemn the trade!![5]

Despite the growing conviction that slavery was evil, it was still legal when the Declaration of Independence was signed.[6] So you think that's hypocritical? You're not alone. Thomas Paine called it flat out "hypocrisy to fight for freedom while maintaining slavery."[7] Are you surprised that this early in American history people were stating these objections? There were others. Author Daniel Mannix states that Patrick Henry held slaves and lamented, "I am drawn along by the general inconvenience of living without them (but) I will not, I cannot, justify it."

Mannix points out that George Washington had similar feelings. Washington told Jefferson that it was "among his first wishes to see some plan adopted by which slavery in his country might be abolished by law."[8]

Jefferson tried to blame the King of England for the institution of slavery in the first writing of the Declaration of Independence.[9] It's like one of the boys saying, "That's the bum that's really promoting this ugly slavery business around here." In this draft, Jefferson stated that King George III, in promoting slavery, "has waged cruel war against human nature itself . . . violating the sacred rights, . . . of a distant people who never offended him."[10]

As you know, this clause never made it into the final form of the Declaration of Independence. You know why? To keep Georgia and South Carolina happy. If the clause were kept in, they threatened to split from the union.[11]

White brothers who were opponents of slavery also emerged in England. One by the name of Thomas Clarkson had a "Damascus road" experience about the issue.[12] While riding on a trip to London, he reported "a direct revelation from God."[13] What did God order him to do? Dedicate his life to wiping out the slave trade.[14] He immediately dismounted, knelt down, and accepted his mission from the Lord.[15]

According to Mannix, Clarkson later joined forces with William Wilberforce, who also despised the cruelty of slavery. The two made a dynamite team. Wilberforce was rich, had political connections, and was an eloquent speaker. Clarkson was a tireless worker, committed to the cause, but wasn't a great spokesman. Together, they were relentless in their fight against slavery. "Wilberforce was challenged to duels" and had his life threatened. He also had his character attacked, and Clarkson was called a "Jacobin white Nigger" by slavery advocates.[16]

Wilberforce, through his position in Parliament, made several attempts to get that legal body to pass laws against slavery.[17] He made very emotional speeches to consider morality above economics.[18] He was voted down each and every time. But he refused to give up.

Finally, in 1807, the British government passed a law which made the trading of slaves "hereby utterly abolished."[19] When the vote was announced, Wilberforce "collapsed," emotionally spent, "weeping in his chair."[20] It is said, that on that day he "received the greatest ovation ever heard in parliament."[21]

THE NEGRO QUESTION

Get the picture? See how God was, early on, working in the conscience of men? With these impassioned pleas from humane men, how did slavery last in America until 1864? And how could they resist the white brothers who cried, "Please don't do this to your fellow man!" and still regard themselves as civilized human beings?

Here's the answer. *Let's make the 'Negro' less than a man, they reasoned.* Or an inferior man. With this viewpoint in place, white domination of black folk would be just, maybe even needed. Ordained by nature itself. The black man would need to be civilized and coddled. Why? He wasn't yet fit to be free. *Ah! Now I feel better.* Or so they thought.

Oops . . . one big problem. How could the black man be inferior if he created civilization? If the black man originally taught and civilized Europe, then their logic for oppressing him is blown to pieces. *Um, let me see.* They got a great idea.

Let's take the civilizations that historically were considered Negro, and "prove" they were really created by white folks. Then the factual obstacles to our "black is inferior" justification will be removed. Sensational plan! Then, we'll camouflage it with scholarship and otherwise good research. Let's use our best minds. Our scholars, because they are white in this environment, will have abundant motivation to promote the scam.

What I have outlined above in my mock portrayal of the thinking of many whites, I will now illustrate from a historical document. I received information on this "gem" while a history student in college. It was given to students to serve as an ideal illustration of a raging social debate. The subject in dispute? The black man's plight in the mid 1800s.

The historical document I'm referring to is a series of magazine articles. The first article was published in December 1849 in *Fraser's Magazine*.[22] It was a racist piece of literature entitled "Occasional Discourse on the Negro Question."[23] The author, a famous, respected intellectual by the name of Thomas Carlyle,[24] was so fond of his article he later expanded it into a pamphlet. He also gave it a brand new title,

The Occasional Discourse on the Nigger Question.[25]

Author Eugene R. August edited and published a small booklet including this article. He also included in the booklet an article by John Stuart Mill, another respected intellectual. Mill's article was written to rebut the racist article written by Carlyle.

August summarizes Carlyle's view, "The perfect society would have the wisest man ruling absolutely at the top, the next wisest in the next position of power, and so on down, with the Negroes at the bottom, just above the domesticated animals."

August goes on to summarize Carlyle's view on another point: ". . . the white race was born wiser than the black race, and thus to emancipate Negroes was only to deprive them of their God-given master."

Does reading those words make you angry? Think about how I felt as a young black man reading this in college. Without having the knowledge I now possess. And at that institution, no one to give me the truth about my people's history. Well, let's move on.

The Carlyle article demonstrates the social and intellectual climate of the time. What I'm going to share with you next is crucial. It will demonstrate vividly why white intellectuals felt the need to destroy the memory of a Negro Egypt.

Here it is. John Stuart Mill, in coming against Carlyle's article, refers to ancient Negro civilization as part of his argument. Eugene August—in summarizing Mill on this point—writes, ". . .the ancient Egyptian civilization was a Negro civilization, . . . the Negro is capable of producing a great culture. . . ."

Interesting. A white intellectual in the mid 1800s, still referring to a Negro Egypt as a historical fact. And not the least bit ashamed of using it to refute a racist. With eloquent men like John Stuart Mill still around, modern Egyptologists proceeded with "one underlying motive."[26] Guess what that was? "To prove that the ancient Egyptians, African Cushites, were not Negroes."[27]

PLAYING THE NAME GAME

In America a group of scholars arose, calling themselves anthropologists. These folks study physical characteristics, racial distributions, environment, social relationships, and culture.[28] They eagerly joined the unholy mission of degrading the Negro. They used Egyptology in such a discriminatory way that one of their members described the work as "niggerology."[29]

Black scholar, Chancellor Williams, informs us that most of African history was written by this kind of anthropologist. Several tactics were employed to blot out black accomplishments. Here is a list of Williams' observations about how the anthropologists chose to operate:

1) "Ignore or refuse to publish any facts of African history" that would not support their racial theories.

2) "Create a religious and 'scientific' doctrine" to ease the white conscience for oppressing and enslaving African people.

3) "Flood the world with hastily thrown together African 'histories'" that contain European perspectives only.

4) Start renaming people and places. "Replace African names of persons, places, and things with Arabic and European names." This will disguise their true black identity.

5) Change the criteria for defining race. For example, one drop of Negro blood in America makes you a Negro, no matter how light your skin. When reporting ancient history, reverse the standard. Make one drop of white blood render someone a Caucasian no matter how dark the skin.

6) When black participation in civilization is so obvious your best schemes can't hide it, find a way to attribute the success to outside white influence.

7) When all the ancient historians contradict your theory, seek to discredit them.[30]

Since the ancient historians, as mentioned earlier, described the Egyptians, Ethiopians, Syrians, Sumerians, and Phoenicians as black folk, new definitions were required. The anthropologist decided black skin, thick lips, woolly hair, and broad noses were insufficient data to make a person a Negro.

Presto! Now we have a new creation. A dark skinned white man with woolly hair. I'll give you a minute to stop laughing.

With the standards and criteria for determining race changed with one swipe of the "magic wand," all kind of games could be played.[31] The regions where black people traditionally lived and reigned suddenly are given a host of all new characters. People show up on the scene who are called "Bantus, Semites, Nilotics, Pygmies, Bushmen, Hottentots, Negroes, Negroids, Caucasians, and Caucasoids."[32] Wow! is that all? Nope. We also get a whole circus full of "'ites,' 'oids,' and 'ics,'" with each portrayed as a distinct race![33]

This kind of foolishness led Stanford professor St. Clair Drake to pose the following two questions. He writes, "Why are people who look like us called 'white' if they live in Egypt but 'Negroes' if they live in this country? And why, if someone of that type turns up among the Egyptian pharaohs is he classified 'white' but if he lived in Mississippi he'd be put in the back of the bus?"[34] Pretty good questions.

Nobody Knows Like Jesus

Hopefully, our objective in this chapter has been achieved. You now possess a basic understanding of why and how the cover-up happened. In chapters two through nine, we gave you some helpful insights and tools for digging up the truth about our people. There is much more that we can learn. For that purpose, we have included a bibliography of helpful books to increase your knowledge. Study them. But remember this. Let the Bible be the final word on all subjects. If you do that, you'll be a winner every time. Accordingly, that's the book you should study the most. It is never wrong and it contains no errors.

We have suffered greatly as a people. Thanks be to God, there are Christian brothers—both black and white—who will come alongside to help us heal our pain. But better than that, there is Jesus. He understands like no one else.

We were great once. At the highest pinnacle of human glory, but now relegated to the bottom of humanity. Jesus understands. He was with His Father in glory and thought it not robbery to be equal with Him. Yet He left the glory of heaven—where He was worshipped and honored by the angels—to become a man. But not just any man. A *doulos* man. A slave. The lowest form of a man. And He did it willingly, without sin, so that He could save you and me.

We were brought so low in our humiliation that the American government once called us 3/5 of a man. Jesus understands. He was God in the flesh. When He was healing the sick and casting out devils, people said He was worse than a man. They called Him a demon. No, worse than a demon. He was called Beelzebub, "the prince of demons."

But they will ask: *If our history was so great, what are we doing at the bottom of modern society?* Jesus understands. They asked of our Savior that if He was truly the Son of God, what was He doing hanging on a cross?

Yes, but people have raped, lynched, and degraded us. Jesus understands. They hung Him on a cross between two thieves. Mocked Him, spat on Him, and gave Him vinegar to drink. Then they buried Him in a borrowed grave.

Yes, brothers Jesus understands. He was down, but not out. Jesus took the grave by the throat and said to death, *get out of my face.* He rose again by His own power and returned to His Father's throne of glory.

Black brothers, now it's time for you to understand. Because you too will return to glory. Unite yourself with Jesus and be glorified with Him. Because it is Jesus and Him only who really deserves to be glorified. And so it shall be. One day every knee shall bow and every tongue will confess that Jesus Christ is Lord to the glory of God the Father (Phil. 2:11)!

TAKING IT DOWN LOW

I've been firing long range jumpers for the whole first half. Busting down lies and deception from 3-point land. But, as many of you know, you can't live on the outside shot alone. You have to take it inside, too. Banging the boards, posting up, and rejecting garbage. "Joel, you're looking hungry, like you're ready to take the game into the trenches. It won't be long now."

Brothers, wouldn't it be nice if the truth could be taught by white and black people together? Side by side. Black preacher Tony Evans expressed it this way. He feels if white Christians, along with black Christians, would teach the truth about black history, it would radically change our country. What a source of healing it would bring to our sick and dying land.

Well brothers, this book represents a contribution to that effort. I

(Don) am an African American, but brother Joel is white. He loves Jesus. And, as you would expect from a true believer, he loves his black brothers. It was his idea to write this book. He wanted the truth contained in these pages to reach the heart of the African American male as much as I did.

Listen to the brother. He is an NBA chaplain and has earned a Ph. D. in pastoral counseling. He has spent countless hours listening and ministering to African American males. He may sound a little corny at times. Like a white man trying to sound black. But his heart is right, and his message is real. Receive the truth he has eagerly waited to bring to you.

God bless you. If I don't see you here on this earth, I'll meet you on the other side. The place where all true warriors end up. The eternal home of men of faith that decide to "Return to Glory."

Time Out

1. What range of emotions did you experience as you read this chapter? How did you handle them?

2. What did the works of Quaker Anthony Benezet, Thomas Clarkson, Count Constantine de Volney, and William Wilberforce say to you about God and your fellowmen from a different race?

3. This chapter talks about Jesus truly identifying with your specific pain. Does this encourage you to go to Him for help? How will you do that?

4. If you are not of African descent, what range of emotions did you experience as you read this chapter? Did you find yourself thinking more time should have been given to whites who fought against slavery? Why?

PART II – THE MENTAL, EMOTIONAL, AND SPIRITUAL ROAD MAP TO WHOLENESS

11 | Comfortable With the Music Off

Well, Don is right. I'm pumped! I have been working with many African American NBA players since 1979 and I'm ready to take this game into the trenches—banging the boards, posting up, and rejecting garbage. We're dealing with some tough stuff at the pro level. We're not messing around. I might be firing some no-look passes in your direction. Are you prepared? What will you do with the ball? Pass it off? Go to the hole? Just stand there?

My brother, Don, has done a great job, hasn't he? Writing about the historical background of anything can be tough—like chewing shredded cardboard. But he made all that potentially dry research come alive! Wouldn't you like to sit down with him for a few hours, discussing what you've already read?

What Don has written begs the question. But where do we take all this? Before we can grasp the bigger picture, we must take an inward journey. There are some things that we must confront.

Many African American men have opened their hearts to me over the years. Some have paused mid-sentence reflectingly, "I can't believe it. What I just told you, I have never shared with another white man."

To be entrusted with the pain of my brothers is an honor. The inward journey we are about to take together has been sponsored by these enlightening talks. Are you ready to try something that everything within you might want to reject?

Go ahead. Try surviving one day without music or any other audio adrenaline. Cold turkey. No Walkman. No TV. No CD blaring in your house driving your momma crazy. No R&B. No LL Cool J. No Salt and Peppa. No Tupac. No "whatever-is-cool-today."

Do you feel the addiction? How would you deal with total silence? Are you comfortable with yourself? Or do you have to keep the radio on?

Does the pounding music keep you from seeing reality as it relates to you and your world?

Can you put your arms around what I am saying? We're not necessarily against listening to music. Generally speaking, music cannot be separated from black culture. Historically, blacks have expressed pain through music. That's just the way it is. But having the constant background noise can serve another purpose. It is important that we look at this before we go on.

Potentially there is a major problem haunting black men—being surrounded by and needing so much external stimulation that the inner man cannot break through. This makes it difficult for a young man to be objective with himself. There is a tendency to stiff arm deeper intimacy with God, ourselves, and others when we continually blast the music. The noise is like a drug that deadens the pain.

It's a paradox. Listen to rap. Listen to the blues. Even though the lyrics say it, the deeper reality we run from is this: Life is tough. Life is about problems. You can talk to any man worth his salt. He'll tell you the same thing. Life is hard.

We all have grown up in a culture that hits us with thirty seconds of propaganda at a time. Beer. Soft drinks. Cars. Shoes. Everybody's having fun. Right? We survey the 'hood and at first glance it looks like two plus two always equals four. Sometimes it's easy to keep acting like life is supposed to be great.

INSTITUTIONAL RACISM

But there is another dimension. Institutional racism. There's no question, it can mess with your mind. Down South it's straight up—we live here, you live there, and let's keep it that way. Up North it's more political, hidden.

In the old days it was well defined. The man didn't like you. You knew exactly what door you could go in and what fountain you could drink from. You had to stay in your place. "Yes Sir, Mr. Smith." But the racism felt today is subtle.

Jim, a high profile professional, told me, "I'm nervous driving down the streets of certain neighborhoods after dark. Not because I might be robbed. I'm afraid of being pulled over by the police."

Every young African American parent deals with when and how to prepare his or her child for the inevitability of racism. Tiesha, the proud mother of three-year-old Darren, watches this cute little "motorcycle in tennis shoes" zip around the yard. She giggles at another one of his antics and then comments matter-of-factly, "You know, he is so cute, but in ten years people will be afraid of him."

And then there's the store manager who watches you like a hawk, finally saying, "If you're not here to shop, leave."

You're unsure of where racism is. It's easy to suspect that racism's everywhere. Of course, some of the stuff that happens isn't racially motivated. People are people, and sometimes people say and do things that are just plain stupid.

Not liking someone because of an abrasive personality style or lack of moral character is understandable. But hating someone sight unseen, just because of the color of the skin is absolutely unreasonable. It's crazy! It's irrational! It's frightening! Racism is the face you put on sin.

Look at what's happened to the hearts of many black men. You can see it. No weeping. No laughing. Shut down. Stone-faced.

The racism that has affected generations of African Americans is not the only situation in the world. A quick look reveals a caste system in India that afflicts literally millions of its poor. And these are people of the same race! Even in Africa, tribalism presents the same type of problems. Recently I read an article that exposed black-on-black slavery in Sudan. Two Baltimore Sun reporters (one black, one white) made an illegal journey to discover this monstrous truth, buying two young brothers and releasing them back to their families.[1]

And speaking of Africa, what about the colonialism that began in the mid 1800s? White Europeans arrogantly looked at Africa as if it were a cake to be cut into pieces. Great Britain, France, Germany, Belgium, Holland, Spain, Portugal, Italy, and Turkey all participated in the mad scramble to dominate that rich land. Settlers came in with an imperialistic attitude, conquering the local people along the way. Anyone with a conscience who has the courage to study this terrible period of human history will weep and then get very angry.

Some things are more unfair than others. Sooner or later, every person discovers this and learns to cope.

DARRELL GREEN, A MAN AFTER GOD'S OWN HEART

Washington Redskins great Darrell Green tells of his arrival in DC as a young, wide-eyed rookie. He was hungry and dropped by a restaurant to grab a bite to eat. The waiter was downright mean. He treated this world-class athlete like a dog. All of a sudden, someone whispered in the waiter's ear, "That's Darrell Green." Shocked and embarrassed, the guy came back over to Darrell and actually apologized for his rudeness. Was the waiter having a bad hair day? Were his actions racially motivated?

We can't climb into the waiter's heart and know the full truth. But Darrell chose to forgive him. If he were speaking to you right now, he'd say, to you as he has discussed with me:

> Racism is a reality. Satan is real. Satan wants to separate people from God. To do this, he must separate them from each other. Sunday morning at 11 a.m. is the most racially divided hour on the planet. It is a reality from both sides of the fence. Signing an anti-racism pledge doesn't do the trick. Nothing like this can be taught logically. There must be an individual revelation from God. Pray for those who despitefully use you. This is hard, but two wrongs don't make a right. Change can only come by each one of us yielding to the Holy Spirit. He is the only One who can change hearts—including mine.

The Glock 9 mm is pointed right at your heart. The $60 million moment-of-truth question is: How do you respond to the unfairness of life? Darrell isn't wearing rose-colored glasses when he says these things. He has experienced life at street level in a single-parent family raised in a poor Houston 'hood. He has gone through the standard stages of reaction to the unfairness of life . . . including racism. He freely admits that he has blown it many times and continues to guard his heart with the Word of God, prayer, and silent meditation on God's promises.

Darrell turned the music off. He has felt the pain of unfairness but refuses to medicate the pain with drugs, alcohol, or sex outside of marriage. He confronted the nasty stuff that gurgled within the cauldron of his heart. Like Darrell, you must take the same journey inward, upward, and outward. It's a lonely trip. No one else can take it for you.

What is involved in that journey? Is it a return to glory? Or are you about to invite more pain? What can you gain from being ruthlessly honest with yourself and God? Turn the page and discover for yourself.

Time Out

1. What kind of music do you listen to? What do the lyrics mean to you? Who are your favorite artists? Why? What do they mean to you?

2. What would it be like for you to spend a whole day alone out in the woods without music, TV, or phone? No external stimulation. Could you do it? Describe what you might be feeling inside.

3. Are you comfortable with yourself when everything else around you is silent? What do you think about? Do you like yourself? What would you change about yourself if you could wave a magic wand and make anything happen? Why?

4. If you were treated like Darrell Green was treated in that restaurant, how would you have reacted? Why?

5. If you are not of African descent, focus on the word *racism*. What images does this word bring to your mind? If your best friend were to ask you if you were racist, what would your answer be? Why? What is your definition of racism?

12 | Culture Shock

Do you remember the last funeral you attended? Who died? Did a friend get caught in a cross-fire and get shot up? Was it a drug overdose? Suicide? Did a relative die of natural causes?

What did you feel when you heard about his or her death? What did you feel a week later? How about six months later? What are you feeling right now as you reflect upon this person and what he or she meant to you?

We deal with a lot of things that are like death to us. It always has to do with loss. We lose friends, jobs, lovers, time, money, body parts, and a bunch of other stuff. If we are gut-level honest with ourselves and don't try to smoke, snort, or drink our sorrow into oblivion, we must face ourselves and what we feel.

In times of serious heartache, every bone and tissue in our body screams out in pain. We never want to hurt this bad again. We look for ways of escape. But if we keep the music off, we are confronted with a terrible problem: We are human. We cannot change the circumstances. What's done is done.

And then the emotional law of gravity kicks in, pulling us down toward the pit. People wiser than you and I tell us that there is a predictable set of emotional reactions that every human being must experience when loss occurs.[1]

NORMAL EMOTIONAL REACTIONS TO LOSS
(The Slippery Slope)

The Moment

Denial

Anger

Bargaining

Acceptance

Fear

The Pit

Depression

Let's talk about the predictable reactions.[2] It doesn't matter how much spiritual or psychological information you have stuffed between your ears. Nor does it matter how old and experienced you are. When loss of any kind strikes, you are taken to school. You are given a crash course in how weak, frail, and vulnerable you are as a human being. And how close we all really are to snapping.

Important. What we are about to discuss is a general overview of what may have happened or is happening to you right now. Sometimes when we discover words that fit our feelings, we say, "Aha, this is it! This is where I was, this is where I am right now, and this is what will help me be a better person for the future!" Your experiences may seem to be somewhat different, but perhaps you will be able to identify with the previous comment after you have reached the end of this book. We are hoping that you'll experience this book as a kind of a road map to wholeness—mentally, emotionally, and spiritually.

Marriage and family counselor Dr. Clarence Walker communicated to me that many African Americans have fluid boundaries. Therefore, it is hard to couch every reader in a rigid model. You might not experience every stage of grief mentioned, but here we go. Ready?

Denial. Anger. Bargaining. Depression. Acceptance. This is not fun. Grieving is hard work. It is a rude awakening. In fact it is down right frightening. You are one hair's breadth away from insanity. And I am as serious as a heart attack.

THE MOMENT

Let's turn a gentle corner together. How does this apply to you and this inward, upward, and outward journey we've been talking about? Take a look at this:

Once riding in old Baltimore,
    Heart filled with glee
I saw a Baltimorean
    kept looking straight at me.
Now I was eight and very small,
    and he was no whit bigger
And so I smiled, but he poked out
    his tongue and called me "Nigger."

I saw the whole of Baltimore
    from May until December:
Of all the things that happened there
    That's all that I remember.
—Author Unknown

Take a deep breath. Exhale slowly. Take a few seconds. Try to remember the first moment you realized that because of your skin color the rules were different somehow for you in this country. How old were you? Where were you? Who was in the room? What were you feeling? Try to capture that feeling right now.

VERBAL SNAPSHOT OF BERNARD'S MOMENT

That moment is indelibly etched in Bernard's mind. Born and raised in southeast Washington, DC, a highly educated and successful businessman, Bernard Jones remembers that moment well. His dad worked on Capitol Hill as a personal assistant to a senator. His mother was a legal secretary. They worked hard to shield their kids from the cruel, harsh realities that awaited them on the outside.

Bernard went to a completely segregated elementary school. All the teachers expected nothing but the best from the five Jones kids. Bernard excelled. He was a "Jones kid."

Right around seventh grade something snapped. He found a magazine that boasted a front cover shot of his school. Bernard was excited, and he took it proudly to show his teacher. "Isn't this great?" His teacher responded with a knowing smile, patted him on the head with a "That's nice, Bernard."

Confused by the tepid response, Bernard took a harder look at the theme across the top: "The Defacto Segregation in American Schools." Whoa! Wait just a minute! Do you mean that my school is an example of something that I'm not supposed to be proud of? And then he noticed that the camera angle from a cluttered alley had pulled a rat into the picture. This was too much. Culture shock.

Bernard states that from that moment of realization he felt the downward pull toward the pit. It was like a cosmic conspiracy. He was faced with social injustices everywhere he turned. He began to experiment with heroin and Ripple wine to kill the pounding pain. A double life: As and Bs in school, church on Sunday, and getting blasted in an abandoned building two blocks away from his house every chance he could.

How could someone like Bernard get out of the pit? Hold on. We'll explore that in a moment.

THE LOSS OF A DREAM

Fred Hickman, the Ace Award-winning sportscaster of CNN's Sports Tonight remembers The Moment. He had grown up in Springfield, Illinois, Abe Lincoln's home town, with both black and white kids as his best friends. It didn't occur to him that there was a difference. When he and his friends moved on to junior high, he was suddenly confronted by white kids who wanted to beat him up. "Huh, what's this all about?"

NFL Hall of Famer, Lenny Moore remembers the strange, uncomfortable feelings he experienced sitting in high school assembly with everyone singing "Old Black Joe."

Investment counselor Roscoe Turner can replay The Moment in vivid detail. At the age of ten he was a member of Philadelphia's All City Boys Choir. One day, dressed in suit and tie, with sheet music tucked under his arm, he was taking the bus home after practice. This particular day, however, he made a mistake. Temporarily confused as to where he was, he got off at the wrong bus stop. The bus took off. A few seconds later he was surrounded by a bunch of white guys who didn't have a clue as to who he was or what he was about. Just because of his skin color, they beat him up really badly.

Truck dispatcher, Kevin Adams remembers The Moment well. As a teenager in the 50s in North Carolina he was excited about something that had just happened and without thinking he went into the local drug store to celebrate with an ice cream soda. He was refused service. This hit him really hard.

Historian, author and family counselor Dr. Clarence Walker doesn't hesitate either. He distinctly remembers The Moment like it was yesterday. He was five years old. It was his first day of kindergarten. He was playing with a toy when a white child came over and grabbed hold of that same toy. Clarence resisted. The white teacher intervened, giving the toy to the other child and making Clarence sit in the corner.

Racism is loss—the loss of a dream. The loss of the fantasy that everything is supposed to be fair with regard to economic justice and opportunity. When a young man or anyone dares to confront his feelings, things get worse before they get better. It is a daily process marked by little steps toward maturity. We all want to grow up, but no one likes the process.

Emotional pain introduces us to the possibility of maturity. But we hate the pain. Why? Because pain lets us know that we are human and that we need God. There is something deep within us that resists that need. It's called pride: "I can ultimately make it on my own intelligence, personality, and all that resumé/obituary-type stuff."

The initial awareness that racism exists and that both barrels are loaded and locked on you just because of the color of your skin is unbelievable. You experience a loss such as those we have just talked about. It is the loss of your innocence. Suddenly you are forced to grow up in a way and at a speed that is extremely uncomfortable. It is the loss of a dream that you didn't even know you had because God programmed you with the unconscious reality that you are loved, esteemed, and appreciated.

Turn the page and we'll follow the journey of a few men through the five steps from denial to acceptance. We'll discover how you can bleed the effects of racism dry for every bit of maturity you can squeeze out of it. Can anything good come out of all this? Is the return to glory possible? Hmmm, good questions.

Time Out

1. Do you remember the last funeral you attended? Who died? What feelings have you experienced since that time?

2. Do you remember the first moment you realized that because of your skin color the rules were somehow different for you? Try to recapture right now what you experienced at that moment.

3. How have you tried to numb the emotional pain when you have hurt over the loss of someone or something? What happens when the numbness wears off and the pain returns?

4. If you are not of African descent, what loss have you experienced? Try to recapture your emotional response. Imagine what it would be like to be treated differently just because of the color of your skin. Take time to really think about this.

13 | The Ultimate Inward Trip

The return to glory is by way of a difficult path. It's called emotional pain. We have already been given the headlines. But what about the fine print?

This path is a slippery slope . . . going down. As you walk this path, remember that these stages of dealing with the unfairness of life are not wrapped up in neat boxes. "Hmmm, let's see. When I am done with anger, I can then move to bargaining, and I'll never get angry about that again." No! A thousand times, no!

It is a slippery slope because the pull is down toward the pit of despair. That pull is seductive. Everything within you will scream, "Why can't we stay here? I hurt so bad!" Blaming and shaming—pointing the finger—will keep you in the pit.

Emotions in the recovery journey typically go down and then up. By turning the music off, confronting your honest feelings about how you do or do not fit into this world dominated by unfairness, you'll feel awful at first. But then you'll turn a corner and your outlook will begin to improve. There will be temporary setbacks along the uphill return to glory, but you are moving in the right direction. Looking at the five-stage illustration, where would you say you are right now?

For the sake of continuity, let's start at the beginning. Ready?

NORMAL EMOTIONAL REACTIONS TO LOSS
(The Slippery Slope)

The Moment

Denial

Anger

Bargaining

Acceptance

Fear

The Pit

Depression

DENIAL

As we have already figured out, sooner or later all human fantasies break down. Why ask why? That's just the way it is. When you've been "kissed" by a Mack truck at 90 mph, the emotional/brain damage you experience puts the body sensory system on overload instantly. In a similar manner, God has arranged an immediate emotional response to protect us from insanity.

When your hand gets crunched in a slammed car door ("OUCH!"), the whole region goes numb for a while. You are protected from the high voltage pain as your body prepares for the healing process. Feeling returns bit by agonizing bit. That's actually good. Because if the numbness remained, you would have an even more serious problem.

Ever been dumped by a girlfriend ("OUCH!")? That is another profound loss, especially if you really loved her and didn't just view her as a sexual conquest. You go through shock. Denial. "No. This can't be true. I refuse to believe it. I feel numb."

Remember Bernard Jones? The reality that his school was being used as a negative example for segregation in American schools was almost too much for him to bear. It was a defining moment. "This can't be happening to me, to us."

If you were on hand at that precise moment and it were possible to hook Bernard's brain up to a meter measuring mental shock, you probably would have seen an amazing phenomenon: Bernard's mind becoming numb while his thoughts were racing out of control. Denying pain is normal.

It is hard to believe that at this very moment in history some people's hatred gets triggered just because of someone else's skin color. It seems too foolish for words.

Denial has been designed by God to help us get through the initial stages of grief over something or someone we have lost. But it also has a flip side. Sometimes we are so convinced that the worst thing for us is to face the pain. We choose to stay in the denial mode for a long time. This keeps us from dealing with the real issues. The numbness remains.

Enter "cool pose." You know what I'm talking about. It's that certain gangsta lean, that limp, that walk, that swagger. It's that stone-faced look. What's the statement? "I'm tough. I'm cool. I'm strong. I don't cry. I'm not affected by my emotions. I'm confident. I'm in charge. I dare you to hit me when I walk out onto the street right in front of your moving vehicle."

You might want to take a look at what really may be happening. What you are projecting can actually be covering up an incredible amount of pain on the inside. You may be holding on to denial in an unhealthy manner. That is something you'll have to wrestle with. And you will.

What keeps us in denial? Fear. "What do people really think about me? How can I be successful when so much is against me that I have no control over? What will my future hold? What will my kids face?" These and hundreds of other fears crash in like a tidal wave with more than we can handle.

We must keep pressing through the process, or fear will hold us hostage in "La-La Land." But our next destination in the inward journey on the road to glory is a problem that challenges any young man with a vision: Anger.

Time Out

1. Explain denial in your own words.

2. How have you experienced denial in your life?

3. What is "cool pose" all about? Do you know when you are doing it and when you're not? What's happening inside you when you are in it?

4. If you are not of African descent, try to grasp what denial would feel like if you were a person of color. Take a look at the following statement and then respond to the question after the statement: "For whites, the biggest challenge to racial conciliation is our insensitivity to the emotional pain experienced by people of color." Do you agree or disagree with this statement? Why?

14 | **Black Rage, Black Power**

Once you realize *Hey, I'm a young black man growing up in white America and it seems like everything is stacked against me,* you're smacked with fear. Many things that have happened in past history will feed that fear. Real life stories from older folks will confirm that while many things have changed, some things will never change. And those things are out of your control.

The more negativity you encounter, the more your fears are verified . . . life really is unfair. This awakening actually is positive. It helps you to break through denial and into the next stage of the grieving process, anger.

NORMAL EMOTIONAL REACTIONS TO LOSS
(The Slippery Slope)

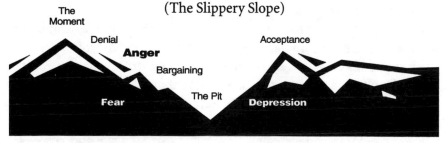

The Moment

Denial

Anger

Bargaining

Acceptance

Fear

The Pit

Depression

ANGER

Anger is a powerful weapon and can be pointed in many directions. Government (There is a conspiracy against us). Churches (These "bless-me" clubs don't address the real needs of our community). Whites (They control my chances for advancement). And so forth. And so on. As time passes, it is natural to become angrier and angrier.

Remember Bernard Jones? He experienced this increasing anger. At 12 years of age, he got mad about the current social injustices—Vietnam, racism, poverty, politics. His anger caused him to study intensely and debate everybody about anything and everything. He was mad enough to chew nails.

The next year he graduated from an all-black elementary school to a mostly white junior high school. He was driven to excel. As one of the top students in his class, he realized for the first time that he could be competitive and be successful in white America.

During this time of academic success, oddly enough, he jumped with both feet into drugs, alcohol, sex, and something else—cars. "I developed a strong interest in cars. Even though I didn't have my license, I learned how to steal and strip cars. I can remember going out at 4 a.m., casing cars on my Washington Post delivery route. By the time I was 14, I could remove the transmission from a car with two wrenches in about 15 minutes. I was good."

FOUR WAYS TO DEAL WITH ANGER

Anger is like jet fuel. As with Bernard, it can drive a person to high levels of achievement; or it can take a more destructive route. In fact there are four basic ways to deal with our anger. The first two are negative. The other two are positive.

1. *Rage.* Put your fist through a wall. Slap your girlfriend around or verbally abuse her. Dominate and intimidate everybody you meet. Let your anger rip through every relationship. Destroy your body with drugs. Don't let anyone get close because they'll disappoint you like everyone else has. Push them before they can push you. Get rid of friends before they get rid of you. You get the picture.

Where does the rage come from? The former slave and ceaseless crusader for abolition, Frederick Douglass, who later became ambassador to Haiti, gave a passionate speech on July 4, 1864, which railed out at the hypocrisy of U.S. citizens' celebrating Independence Day while there were still laws on the southern books which were demeaning to blacks. His speech and other writings give us a snapshot of what black people endured in the 1800s.

African American men have a tremendous amount of rage, including a generational transfer of rage. Many young black men are angry and don't quite know why. Regular history classes don't capture the stark brutality of the slave trade, and much of the information presented continues the conspiracy of silence on this matter. It is easy, almost under-standable if you blindly let this rage kick into high gear. Burn a building. Join a gang.

2. *Repression.* A nicer option? I don't think so. "How are you doing?" To that question we respond through clenched teeth, "Oh, just fine." And if we're Christians we'll add, "Praise the Lord." Meanwhile, we bottle this anger in the pits of our stomachs. Someone once said that successful middle class blacks must be successful at one thing—containing rage. It has been called "the rage of the privileged class."

Anger is energy, and it has to go somewhere. If it is internalized, it will reduce your body's ability to defend itself from disease, stress, and fatigue. You may be knocking years off your life and not even know it.

3. *Redirection.* Thankfully, there is a better approach. How about redirecting your anger into something positive or productive. Usually, the best place to start is to go to the person you are angry with and resolve the problem. But when you are angry at the whole white race or society at large, it is difficult to know where to start.

> STEP 1. Pour out your unvarnished rage on paper. Fill a legal pad with everything you are experiencing. Everything. This may take weeks or even months to touch all the bases. Make a copy. Seal the original in an envelope. This may sound corny, but take the photocopy to your back-yard and burn it as a spiritual sacrifice to the Lord while thinking about how God promised to give you "a crown of beauty instead of ashes, (and) the oil of gladness instead of mourning ..." (Isaiah 61:3 NIV). Every anniversary of that date that goes by, read the original copy and write your reflections. You will be amazed as you chart your growth and maturity over the years. This will build your faith. I guarantee.

> STEP 2. Start small. Pump iron. Build muscles. Learn karate. Finish school and do the best you can. Play sports. Be the best worker on your job. Start a hobby. After a few months you'll be able to see some accom-plishments that will put a big smile on your face. Turn your angry energy into something positive. Redirect.

> STEP 3. Invest in people. You can be so fit that you proudly show off your abdominal muscles, which bulge and writhe beneath a thin, sweaty layer of skin, so that you look like you are smuggling pythons down there. But

there is a limit to the satisfaction this can bring. Sooner or later you must get involved in the lives of other people.

An example of Step 3 is Dr. Clarence Walker. If anybody has the right to live in frozen rage, it's Clarence. He grew up with his grandparents in the tough section of North Philadelphia. His alcoholic father was absent, and his mother was sick. In spite of being surrounded by dysfunction in his family, gang warfare, and racism at every turn, Clarence has come through as pure gold. He remembers his grandmother singing hymns around the house. His grandparents were survivors and they lived with strong Christian values behind closed doors. They taught him to never quit. Keep on keeping on. Keep pushing.

After years of education, Dr. Walker formed Philadelphia's first interracial youth advisory committee to inform the mayor of ways to address problems in the inner city. Since then Clarence has been in private practice as a licensed marriage and family counselor specializing in the issues that confront African Americans. He has spent his life working through his anger and redirecting his energies to help thousands of others. In fact, many of the ideas and concepts for this book have been birthed in Dr. Walker's heart. Don and I and you, the reader, can be thankful for his determination to follow Jesus over the years.

Take your pain to Jesus and let Him surprise you with some incredible ways to reach out to others who may be struggling with the very same problem you are dealing with.

Caution: Don't rush into helping others too soon. You may burn out and not help anyone. Time is your best friend if you have a plan. Start your redirection in small, personal ways.

4. *Resolution.* This is our ultimate goal. If you are understanding some new things about your feelings for the first time, you may not be able to resolve things right now. It will take time. We will grab hold of this part of the process later on when we talk about acceptance.

Time Out

1. What makes you angry? How do other people know you are angry?

2. Have you ever felt pure out-of-control rage? How did you express it? How did you feel as it was happening? How about later?

3. How has repression worked in your life? How has it affected you on the inside?

4. Have you redirected your anger? How?

5. Set aside time to go through Step 1, writing out your feelings on paper. Go through the whole process, giving those feelings to God. Know that He listens and cares.

6. If you are not of African descent, take a hard look at the anger experienced by young black men. Quick, what is the first thought that pops into your mind? What surprises you most about that thought? Why?

15 | Let's Make a Deal

How are you doing? Heavy stuff, huh? Before going too much farther, let's again make something clear. These five stages don't always happen in the order we've been talking about. "Hmmm, I'm done with anger. Isn't that nice? Now what?"

Once you have confronted the unfairness of your situation, you could jump from denial to bargaining and then roar back to anger and park there for a few years. In fact you could cruise through all five stages in a single day and be right back where you started the next morning. How's that for a trip?

NORMAL EMOTIONAL REACTIONS TO LOSS
(The Slippery Slope)

The
Moment

Denial

Anger

Acceptance

Bargaining

Fear

The Pit

Depression

BARGAINING

But what is bargaining? Note the illustration It is the third stage in working through the process of dealing with the unfairness of life as we get back on the road to glory. We haven't hit the pit at the bottom yet. Bargaining can be best understood by two phrases:

• Trying to discover a simple solution to a complex problem.

• Trying to find a quick solution to a long-standing, deeply ingrained problem.

The problem of racism is almost overwhelming. In our American history we have 100 years of slavery and after slavery another 100 years of legally enforced apartheid. This is a complex problem that has vexed thinkers and activists for centuries.

Any quick solutions? Let's try to figure this out. Which political ideology contains realistic, enduring solutions to these issues anywhere in the world? Marxism? Capitalism? Which political party can effectively change racism in America? Democrats? Republicans? Independents? Which religion has the final answer? Christianity? Islam? Judaism? Buddhism? Atheism?

Get the picture? This is tough stuff.

BERNARD'S BARGAIN

Bernard Jones discovered that denial wasn't helping, and his anger only made things worse. How could he make this pain go away?

Bernard moved away from home at 17, attending a college in Kentucky under an early entry program. His only other option was Vietnam, and he wasn't too excited about going there. He was young. The college experience was intimidating, expensive, and consumed all of his time. This change forced him out of the drug scene real quick. The second year he found a job at a local furniture company and immediately moved off campus.

By 18 years of age, he was promoted to warehouse supervisor, managing a bunch of middle aged workers. The reality of social injustices plagued him even more as he studied. He was a thinker, asking a ton of questions. One professor gave him reasons why Christianity didn't seem to work. He swallowed that information hook, line, and sinker.

Other students noticed his leadership qualities, and before long he was voted president of the student government. His thought was that he could bring greater quality to student life and to his world if he could move the political process. Soon he became a die-hard Marxist-Leninist, influenced by the Black Panthers and Communism. He thought about Cuba. About starting a revolution. Torch and burn. The only solution was to destroy the old and then build a new country, a new leadership. Quick fix for complex problems? Bargaining?

SEARCHING FOR SOLUTIONS

His political science professor took Bernard and a couple of others to

Africa the summer after his junior year. What an opportunity to meet and learn from some revolutionaries in Liberia, Ghana, Sierra Leone, and Nigeria! The reverse discrimination was neat. Whites were singled out in customs with long delays and thorough bag searches. For Bernard's group, it was refreshingly different. "Welcome, brothers. Walk right over here through customs. No problem." What a great feeling!

During the visit, he met black Americans of all types. Some were "Uncle Toms," driving around in Mercedes-Benzes with no regard for the poverty all around them. This was a wake-up call for Bernard. Others were in traditional dress, trying to help the best they could.

The revolutionaries were either atheists or followers of Islam. He had some fascinating dialogues with them. The main message, however, that he took away from them was, "There is the need for economic development without tearing everything down."

Coming back to America was a challenge. He definitely wanted to live in Africa. He returned to the furniture company during his senior year, was promoted to the front office, and began hiring blacks.

Still as a devout Marxist, he was becoming intrigued with the other side of the coin: Capitalism. Making money. He learned this on the job, not in the classroom. Some philosophies that thrive in a closed class-room setting don't fly in real life. With all of its weaknesses, business enterprise made sense to him. He intuitively knew that the business world was where he was going to make his mark.

If, in the future, he encountered subtle or blatant racism, he would beat the system with this attitude, "My boss is racist? That may be the reality and I'll deal with that. But I am just thankful to have a job. What my boss is doing is human nature. The fact is that whoever is in control, whether black, brown, red, yellow, or white, the tendency is to deal with their own kind in a more favorable light. I'll work through the system and someday I'll own my own company and then I can do what I want."

Bernard still had to deal with the slippery slope of working through the process. Denial and anger were still waiting at his back door. His bargaining involved the search for a quick solution to the racial problems. He resolved to fight in a more positive way, through business endeavors. But there was still a hole. A gap in his understanding. The only way to discover the full answer was to go into the pit. He didn't go willingly.

There were heels marks and signs of giant struggle all the way down.

To be with Bernard now is an incredible experience. He has spent more than his fair share of time in the pit and has worked through the major challenges presented by his anger. He is an honest struggler. Bernard hasn't arrived by a long shot, but he has redirected his energies to mentor many young men as they chart their own way through the grieving process. He is an inspiration!

Let's go over to the edge of the pit together. Do you want to go in or do you want to turn and run? Turn the page and we'll hook up with Ferdie Johnson, a guy you might identify with in some way. He'll lead the way.

Time Out

1. What have you considered as you have looked for quick solutions to the problems of racism? If you are not of African descent, take a look at the same question.

2. Have you talked with God regarding racism? What have you asked of Him? Has this bargaining process hurt or helped your relationship with God?

3. How do you feel about God right now?

4. What stupid mistakes do you need to watch out for in this bargaining stage? What, if any, mistakes have you already made? What did you learn? How can you reach out to others who may be making the same mistakes?

16 | The Pit of Despair

It is utterly exhausting being black in America, physically, mentally and emotionally.

Marian Wright Edelman
Director, Children's Defense Fund

Depression. Anger turned inward. Frozen rage. The pit. Sounds like a fun way to spend an afternoon? A week? A year? A lifetime? I don't think so.

What happens when you can't bargain your way around the problems of racism in this world? What happens when you discover that your intellect, your spit and vinegar, your personality style and enthusiasm don't amount to a hill of beans. It's like going to the ocean and trying to command the crashing waves to stop doing what they're doing. Some claw their way back to denial or anger. But many slide down to the pit of depression. Thud. They hit bottom.

Have you ever been there? If you have, you'll agree that it is almost impossible to describe the full range of unbearable emotion. Hopelessness. Perhaps you may think,

> *Everything I have tried to do in a positive manner has failed. What is my place on this planet? I can't slick-talk my way through this stuff. Politics doesn't work. Religion is filled with self-serving hypocrites. Business enterprise is filled with 'Destination Sickness.' It's empty once you get there and have it all. Absolutely nothing I can do will make a difference. I think I'll just give up.*

Does this sound too dramatic? C'mon, you can roll your eyes, *Puhleeeze. Give me a break!* If you have never really hit bottom in anything, you will not be able to relate. All this may seem out of touch with where you are. Stick with me.

NORMAL EMOTIONAL REACTIONS TO LOSS
(The Slippery Slope)

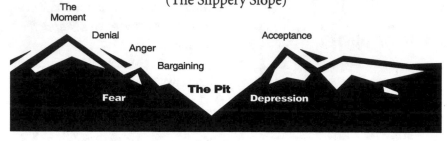

THE PIT EXPERIENCE

Sooner or later you will hit the pit. That's not a threat. It's a promise. Whether it's sports, school, girls, or work, it doesn't matter. Sooner or later you will smack into a brick wall. You'll be knocked silly, like a cartoon character, hearing chirping noises and seeing stars. Perhaps you will then remember what you are reading right now. Maybe not.

Ferdie Johnson, an investment analyst from Charlotte, North Carolina, was a strong nut to crack. Ferdie grew up in poverty in a single mother family with three other brothers. His family had almost no connection with other relatives, and he had minimal contact with church after he was seven years old. As the middle child, he was greatly influenced by his mother's boyfriends and older brothers. They introduced him to drugs, drinking, pornography, skipping school, and fast girls.

It was amazing that he made it to the eighth grade. It was there that one of his teachers, Mr. Olsen, saw his tremendous potential and offered to tutor him after school. To this day Ferdie doesn't know why he accepted the offer. But he did. His desire to learn soon outweighed the bad influence of his brothers. It was tough, though. They continually mocked him and his study habits.

At thirteen years of age, he realized that his brain power would help him succeed in life. He worked his way through high school at a fast food restaurant, studying every spare moment. He aced high school with honors. Fisk University wanted him.

Four years later he graduated from Fisk, returning from Nashville to Charlotte. Major boredom that summer caused him to visit some friends in Atlanta. One of the guys was going to school to become an investment banker. Ferdie was interested in the program. He applied and was accepted. He moved in with a couple of guys, found a job, and started school that Fall.

Next Spring, the local office of a huge investment firm allowed him to work part time. By the time he finished school he was given a junior position in the firm.

Things were going great! He had his own apartment. His life was full. One of the things he discovered was the power successful black men have over black women. He had several women on the string. Like his peers, he dominated them and used them to fulfill his desires. There was no physical abuse or anything like that. It's just that there were so many available women that he could be as committed as he wanted to be, on his terms. Even though the women seemed to be comfortable with sharing him, many were hurt by his selfishness.

At the time, all he was concerned about was his personal happiness. He did not understand it right then, but he was using sexual conquest as a way to dull the pain that was lurking far beneath the surface of his success. He had a good thing going and the women were willing participants. Why not? Right?

NEW YORK CITY

In 1982, Ferdie was offered a high-pressure, responsible position in New York City at the headquarters of the firm. He leaped at the chance.

In New York it struck. Loneliness. He didn't have friends and he was working crazy hours, too hard to make or keep any real friends. No women to make him feel masculine. Besides, in New York it was hard to trust . . . maybe that girl really was a guy! But he hadn't quite reached bottom, yet.

New York is an expensive place to live, but he found an apartment about twenty minutes from his office. Every day the void he felt within got bigger and bigger. The busyness of his job couldn't fill it. He had no way of knowing how vulnerable he was. He was a 29-year-old, well-dressed professional with an empty heart. He had had no real role models since Mr. Olsen in eighth grade. There was no one to talk to about man-to-man things. If he had been a tree, a good stiff wind could've blown him over. He didn't know it. But he was an accident looking for a place to happen.

Late one evening he left his office with a bulging briefcase to do the same old return-to-the-apartment-and-work-some-more-but-don't-forget-the-milk-and-bread ritual. While waiting for the light to change at one of the street corners, a guy standing next to him made casual conversation and then asked him if he wanted some cocaine.

Whoa! What a shock! It was as if someone had smacked him. He hadn't even considered drugs for years. His life had been too full. But at this moment he felt his head nod up and down. They crossed the street together. His heart raced. With furtive glances around they made the transaction.

Back at the apartment, he laid back in the easy chair, permitting the drug to take over. Exhilarating. Technicolor.

As the months passed, he became hooked. Drugs devoured much of his money. His performance on the job didn't seem to suffer initially. A little slip-up here. A little forgetfulness there. But by the end of that year, his boss was beginning to wonder what was happening to Ferdie.

He called Ferdie in for a meeting. "What's going on? You're not the same man that I hired." Ferdie was able to verbally dance his way through the situation for the moment, but it was a wakeup call.

Two days later he got the message that his youngest brother had been killed in a motorcycle accident. He went back to Charlotte that weekend for the funeral. He cried and cried till he thought there could be no tears left. This hit him right between the eyes!

He spent much of the next day alone in his hotel room reading the Gideon Bible that had been placed there. Around 2:30 that afternoon he surrendered his life, his emptiness, his career, his problems, his addiction to cocaine, and his heart to Jesus Christ. "Jesus, I know that I am a sinner. I also know that You died on the cross for my sins. Please come into my life, forgive me for my sins and take over. Please fill me with Your Holy Spirit." It was like a giant weight fell off his back.

But this was just the beginning. Back in New York he went to his boss and admitted to his drug problem. A huge risk. But he instinctively knew that the only way for him to deal with the dark secrecy of his problem was to shed light upon it and make himself accountable, not only to God, but to some human beings who could "hold his feet to the fire." He had to accept responsibility for what he had done wrong, regardless of the cost. Thankfully, the firm had a rehab program. His boss was behind him all the way.

Up to this stage, his focus had been on everyone and everything else. "The government is so out of touch. . . ." "Those hypocritical Christians, they. . . ." "If only he hadn't. . . ." Even though, to many casual observers, he was considered to be a self-made man, blaming and shaming had been the subtext of much of his life.

But now at the rehab center he had a lot of time to reflect. He had hit rock bottom. It was a time of intense self-examination. Ferdie was alone for hours every day. He was plagued with powerful images of personal failure like never before. He confronted the self-destructive, I-don't-deserve-any-form-of-success root in his life. Checking. Cross-checking. Taking inventory. Confronting the anger directed toward himself and others. Challenging excuses he had harbored and nurtured for years. Crying out to God, hoping He was listening.

Even though Ferdie had been exposed to Christianity at a young age he didn't have a clear understanding of God's amazing grace. It was during this period that God began to grab his full attention with a few Christian ministers teaching about the Bible on local radio.

For the first time, he was sensitive to the intense suffering Jesus endured for his sins. He committed his life to Jesus in a brand new way. Knowing full well that the unfairness of life may even get worse, Ferdie committed his life to Jesus like he had never done before. He was well on his way to the next and most exciting part of a life-long process.

By the way, Ferdie has been drug free for nine years now. He is married and has two kids. The firm kept his job for him and has responded to his performance with several promotions. He is painfully aware of his addictive tendencies and has set up people and principles around his life to guard and protect himself from the seductive whisper of temptation. Hang around Ferdie for a few minutes and you're touched by his contagious enthusiasm. He doesn't even have to say it. You know it. He loves Jesus Christ with all his heart.

With teeth gritted in dogged determination and eyes blazing with eternal purpose, Olympic gold medalist and NBA great, David Robinson says it all, "I would die for what I believe. I know Jesus Christ. I know about the motivation for my life. If I'm not willing to give up my life for the Lord, then there's nothing else in my life worth standing for. And I have that kind of conviction in the way I live."

Ferdie agrees.

Time Out

1. Have you ever been in the pit? What happened?

2. What in Ferdie's experience do you relate to? Why?

3. Reread David Robinson's statement. Could you say the same thing and mean it? Why?

17 | Young Warriors

You are a warrior. A fighter smack dab in the middle of a concrete jungle. You are no door mat. No way. You weren't designed to be walked on by anybody or trampled by anything.

As an intelligent warrior you have seen the real enemy, and that enemy is you. You grabbed Denial by its throat and exposed it for what it is . . . an image without substance.

Anger tried to sink its deadly claws into your chest, but you felt the havoc it was trying to wreak in your life. With veins popping in your neck and teeth clenched, you let out a blood-curdling scream, flinging it violently away from you.

The smooth operator, Bargaining, glided effortlessly into your space with a quick fix. BIP! WAP! BAM! You blew it away with military precision.

Now a thick, dark cloud moves in over you. You are helpless under its power. Depression throws you into a pit. "You, a warrior?" it mocks. "You're a worthless piece of garbage. You will never amount to anything. Just look at you. Give it up." Suddenly, a shaft of light penetrates the smog. A strong hand reaches down. In that surreal moment you notice a scar. With little strength left, you lift your arm. The hand grabs yours and lifts. You are mesmerized. You feel nothing but love. Yet you are gazing into the eyes of the fiercest, *baddest* Warrior of all time, Jesus Christ. The acceptance you experience in His presence gives you the boost you need to accept yourself and your circumstances.

ACCEPTANCE

This is what it's all about. Isn't it? Taking a cold hard look at yourself and then developing a positive action plan. We have already discovered and accepted the fact that everybody has problems and is confronted with unfairness on a daily basis. We also have determined that the predictable reactions to those problems are as old as Adam and Eve. Becoming the

119

master of your reactions through help from the master warrior, Jesus, is the most important step in this final stage, Acceptance. He promises to cover your back while you courageously do battle with some giant monsters in your life.

NORMAL EMOTIONAL REACTIONS TO LOSS
(The Slippery Slope)

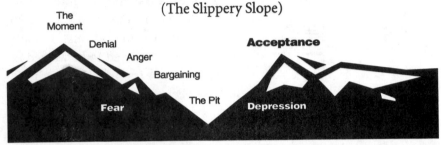

Acceptance is not resignation. Ever felt the pull toward resignation? "Nothing's going to change. I'm not going to change. I might as well quit trying. Nobody knows the trouble I've seen. It's hopeless. There are always going to be racial problems. I've already got two strikes against me, anyway. Why bother to get fired up about any of this stuff?"

Resignation is the language of the pit. The kind of talk that brings yourself and everybody else down. A defeatist mentality. The way a professional victim would think. It's giving in, giving up. As a warrior you have no other alternative but to destroy this attitude before it devours you. Listen to Richard Bolles as he talks about the *Victim Mentality:*[1]

> The Victim Mentality ultimately discharges you from any responsibility in your life, since clearly what is happening to you is not your fault. You don't have to lift a finger. Things which suggest you can take initiative, and actually change your life—are clearly for other people, who aren't up against what you're up against. So runs the Victim Mentality. . . .

> There is a vast difference between being a victim (which we all are, in some areas of our life) and having the Victim Mentality. Being a victim means there are some areas of my life where I am battling powerful forces, but I still do battle with them. Whereas, having the Victim Mentality means giving up: *What's the use? Why even try? I have no power at all; the things you suggest may help other people, but they can't offer any hope to me.*

I want to state a simple truth, and that is, I believe every individual has more control over his or her life than he or she thinks is the case. I have seen dramatic examples of this. . . .

Talk is cheap. It's easier said than done. In fact most people claim to be in the acceptance stage long before they actually are. We usually think we have arrived. But all of a sudden something hits us from our blind side and knocks us down the slippery slope again. There is, however, a way to protect yourself.

Acceptance is feisty. As warriors we fight back. Acceptance is part of the fight. But we must fight with the right weapons, for the right purpose, with the right enemy in focus.

But who is the real enemy? The Ku Klux Klan? Society? Apathetic people? Government? Religion? Educators? Satan?

Well, yes, Satan and his demons are absolutely committed to our destruction. No question, the devil is our ultimate foe. But Satan's head was crushed at the cross when Jesus, the Warrior Lamb, fought and won the greatest battle ever fought. When we lend Satan our minds, only then can he influence our thinking. His head has been smashed. Even the weakest man can blow Lucifer away with a simple prayer of faith. We got the Warrior Power. The real enemy is you. Your attitude . . . stinkin' thinkin'.

The real weapons are invisible—faith in what Jesus did on Calvary for you and faith in what the Bible says. Faith is like a telescope. It brings the heavenly object into clearer view. The real purpose for choosing to live in acceptance is to bring honor and glory to the Ultimate Warrior, Jesus. Isn't it going to be great to meet Him face to face? Can't wait! Can you?

Successful publisher, entrepreneur, and co-warrior, Terry Millender, has dealt with similar issues as an elite army honor guard at the Tomb of the Unknown Soldier. In his life he has stumbled through the five stages. He has chosen to live in acceptance and build his dreams on solid ground. But it hasn't been easy.

Terry wastes no time when asked for his views about acceptance. "For years I was a domestic nomad, wandering around in 'my own back-yard' looking for validation in all the wrong places. I didn't grow up in Africa. I grew up in America. I am more action oriented. I don't want to waste my time reacting to the negative social climate. That's not my focus. I can't control people, what they think or say about me and my race. I can't control the social climate. But I can control my attitude and I can change my responses to unfair situations. I have found my place in society, and I am making a positive contribution."

PERSONAL RESPONSIBILITY

Take a look at what Terry is saying. What is your responsibility? What do you have control over? In fact it might be a good thing to sit down and make a list of such things. I'll start you off: attitude, body language, what you say, when and how you say it. Get the picture? These are things that nobody else can do for you or make you do. Right?

Now make a list of things you have absolutely no control over. This list could go on forever . . . like thunder and lightning and other weather stuff. Not that, though. Just list the things you can't control in terms of human relationships. How about the way people think about you? Or what people say about you when you're out of the room?

The more you put your focus on the things you *can't* change, the more you are setting yourself up to become more bitter and angry. But the more you set your sights on what you *can* control, the more you experience peace and quietness within. This takes the courage of a warrior committed to obey the Master Warrior every step of the way.

Our emotions pay the price of what our mind is thinking. If our thinking is unrealistic, our emotions will hit the dirt.

By the way, choose your friends wisely. Who you hang with will determine your state of mind more than anything else. You won't even have to get rid of negative influences. Try an experiment. Start changing your thinking with God's help and watch to see who still hangs with you and who leaves. You will be amazed.

Happiness and depression never mix. It's called the Lottery Mentality. We feel the emotion of happiness if our circumstances are just right. But the cloud of brooding bitterness washes over us when things don't go our way. We don't take responsibility for ourselves. We're always reacting to the actions of others or waiting for something good to happen to us.

Joy and sorrow mix all the time. It's called the Warrior Mentality. Ask Bernard Jones. If he were here right now he'd tell you that he still feels the pain, the sorrow. But he knows that the Master Warrior has taken all of us to another level, if we dare to follow. And Bernard has courageously followed. It is at this higher level that we fully realize life is not fair, but that we refuse to blame and shame our way through life. Rather, we choose to think differently. Like Bernard, Terry, Darrell, Fred, Clarence, and so many other brothers, do you have the courage to live at this level?

Are you a true warrior? Are you a real man? What will be important 1,000 years from now, or even 20 years from now?

Think clearly and you'll feel clearly. That's joy even in the face of social injustice. Now you are ready to discover your purpose for being here and why your unique circumstances make you a warrior with incredible potential. To have suffered much is like knowing many languages. It gives the sufferer access to many more people.

Time Out

1. What does it mean to be a warrior?

2. In your own words, what is the difference between acceptance and resignation? What is the difference between being a victim and the Victim Mentality? Which way do you lean? How do you know?

3. Make a list of things you *cannot* control. What do you feel as you look over the list?

4. Make a list of things you *can* control. What can you change about yourself? How will you do it? Who around you will help keep you honest as you make the change?

5. Reflect on this statement: Happiness and depression never mix, but joy and sorrow mix all the time. Do you agree? Why?

6. Think of a recent decision you made. What about that decision will be important 1,000 years from now? What is it about you and the way you live your life that puts a big fat smile on Jesus' face?

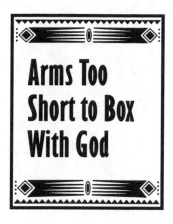

18 | Arms Too Short to Box With God

A little story. The kite was flying so high that he could see for miles. This was not like other days, though. He was getting bored with the same view of the tall buildings, the trees, and the park. He became frustrated and wanted his freedom.

The kite looked at the string and began to think. *This string is holding me back. I can't explore. I can't do my own thing. I can't do the things that fulfill me and make me happy. In fact, I can't do anything I want to do. This is ridiculous. I'm not going to take this anymore. I think I'll cut myself free.*

So the kite did just that.

He cut the string.

He crashed.

Moral of the little story. You are the kite. God has designed you to fly high. He has also put some string, some restraints, in your life: Parents. Teachers. Coaches. Pastors. Counselors. Police. Speed limits. Civil laws. Your family. The ten commandments. The Holy Spirit. The Bible.

Like the string attached to the kite, with the tension of things pulling you back, you can use the winds, the problems that blow against you, to fly high. The moment you cut the string, you crash and burn. No string. No wind. No fulfillment of dreams.

It is your choice. God's grace will help you. You can choose to fight against this truth, but your arms are too short to box with God.

19 | Grass and Concrete

You've seen it. Grass growing through concrete. Those tender shoots are tough enough to crack three inches of cement.

Think of all the social injustice and unfairness of life as concrete that has been poured over you long before you were even born. Think of yourself as the grass. Ain't nothin' gonna keep you down! Right? You'll force a crack in the system, poke your head through.... "Here I am, all you lucky people!"

How can you find meaning in life? How can you make your mark and then help others on their return to glory? What are you here for? How do you bust through the concrete?

Richard Bolles put together an interesting concept in his book, *The Three Boxes of Life.* He said that there are three dimensions to life: learning, working, playing.[1] Of course, there is a fourth dimension . . . the spiritual dimension. We'll talk about that in a moment.

Most of life is in these three boxes. As youngsters, we spend 80 percent of our time learning at school and at home. As adults, we spend 80 percent of our time working. Once we retire, we spend 80 percent of our time playing. We tend to live out of balance. We need to learn how to combine these experiences to achieve balance.

The myth is that only Michael Jordan can be in all three boxes at the same time. What a big mistake! Some think that you can't be in all three boxes at once unless you are an unusually gifted artist, athlete, or entertainer. It is easy to believe the myth that we can't find "Michael Jordan, Will Smith-type" work.

What Bolles suggests is to discover the skills you already have by identifying the "Magnificent Seven"—the seven most enjoyed or satisfying accomplishments in your life. Close your eyes and try to remember what you have enjoyed the most. A part-time job? Volunteer work? Extracurricular activity? Something you learned to do, which once you could not do? List all the things you have ever enjoyed doing, at work, at play, or while learning; and then pick the "Magnificent Seven."[2]

Discipline yourself to sit down and write an essay of at least two pages about each experience. An interesting pattern will begin to emerge. Heads-up questions: What would you do if making money was not an issue? (Just hanging out would get real boring real quick.) What would you be doing? What are you passionate about?

At most high school graduation exercises, the speaker will say something like, "The world of careers before you is infinite." I know what they are trying to say, but that statement is wrong. Your choices are limited. At the high school level you are faced with only three options: college, military, or McDonald's! But once you have determined who you are in terms of functional skills, you are wide open for the next step.

Now you are ready to turn to the world of work. Richard Bolles says that there are People jobs (teacher/sales), Information jobs (computers/accountant), and Thing jobs (aircraft/auto mechanic).[3] You define the options, realize what they are, and then begin to move in that direction.

Take a look at the "Hoop Dreams" syndrome. Out of 700,000 boys who play high school basketball, only 15,000 make it to the college level. Of that number only 200 are drafted by the pros. Only 50 of those ever play a minute in the NBA.[4] The percentages are about the same for other sports as well. Dream big, guys. But don't ignore reality. As NBA players often say, "Stay in school. It's your best move."

Your goal here is to find something that fills all three boxes. A job where you're constantly learning and growing. Where you're earning money to put some meat and potatoes on your dinner plate. But at the same time you are having a blast. *They pay me to do this?*

There is a new power and freedom that automatically follows you once you understand what motivates and drives you. You have turned the music off and have gotten down to the core of your being. Now the Holy Spirit begins to work. Remember that fourth dimension?

THE "SIROCCO EFFECT"

My buddy Robert calls this the "Sirocco Effect." How so? Well, soon after he was married, he and his wife moved to Indiana. They needed a new, used car. He went car shopping. He wanted the American dream. A good car. Low mileage. No clanking noises under the hood. For under a thousand bucks. Lots of luck, right? He wasn't looking for a particular brand or model.

He found a VW Sirocco that met his expectations. He had never heard of a Sirocco prior to this. This was not an issue. He just wanted a decent vehicle. As he drove it around, Siroccos began to appear everywhere!

Like what happened to Robert, the moment you get inside your dream and begin to live it you will see it everywhere! What turns you on? Photography? Cameras? You're into it. You're good at it. You study it every chance you get. You've accepted it as your passion.

You walk down the hallway at school. Normally you'd zip right by the bulletin board. But this time an ad catches your eye, "Photo Assistant Needed at Local Newspaper."

Your mom drags you to Uncle Ralph's retirement party. You don't want to be there. Half way through the evening you discover that your third cousin works at a photo lab which has an entry level position available. *This is too much of a coincidence!*

You are now operating out of your gifts, interests, and talents. We miss the blessing when we try to conform to the boys in the 'hood who say, "Making money or chilling is more important than working and living out your dream." Follow your dream. The money and the leisure will be included in the package.

Quick story. There was a young man who wanted to get the best of his teacher. The student planned a trick he believed he could not lose. He told a friend, "I have a bird in my hands. I will ask my teacher if it is dead or alive. If he tells me it is alive, I will crush it. If he tells me it is dead, I will open my hands and let it fly away. Either way, I will win."

The young man approached his elderly teacher with this question . . . and held his breath as he awaited the anticipated response. But the wise teacher was very calm and said, "My son, whether this bird is alive or dead is entirely in your hands."

Your future is in your hands. Take time to grasp this profound reality. You are ready to stop focusing on the concrete—the problems that are trying to squash you. Government. Politics. Economics. White America. You have discovered that anger clouds your judgment. You are "vision driven," not "anger driven." It's your vision. Like any good vision, it will die and then will be resurrected in God's time. But you knew that. You don't get caught up with anger. You might slip down the slope momentarily when confronted by some insensitive pig, but you jump back into your vision quickly. The concrete is just there. It always has been and always will be. It doesn't threaten you or your masculinity. Wait a minute. Masculinity? What's that all about and how does that fit into your personal return to glory?

Time Out

1. How does your life relate to a blade of grass growing through a crack in the concrete?

2. Make a list of the seven greatest experiences in your life and write a two-page essay on each experience. It is worthwhile to go to your local library and borrow Richard Bolles' book, *The Three Boxes of Life*. He will lead you on a far deeper journey on this subject.

3. In your own words, describe the difference between being "vision driven" and being "anger driven." Explain how anger can cloud someone's judgment? How do you know when you are "vision driven"?

20 | Boyz to Men

Check out the latest shoot-em-up gangsta movie and you'll see real men in action. Right? They don't cry. They don't show weakness. They are unpredictable. They get what they want. Other people are kind of in awe of them, maybe even scared of them. These guys seem to like it that way.

Burping and swearing aside, what's your idea of a real man? Have you seriously sat down, turned the music off, and thought about this at street level? What is a true man?

Bone from California says, "You can't let a guy step on your shoe and just walk away. The homeboys'll think you a buster (coward)."

"First time I put the gun on somebody," says Iceman from Illinois, "and took the stuff, man, my (gang) was giving me five, and saying, 'you great, you the man.' It was, like, they loved me and stuff...."

Before going too much farther, let's establish eye contact with a few searching questions: Who is your real-life (not a celebrity-type) male hero? How well do you know him? What do you talk about when you are with him? Why did you choose this particular man? How have you tried to pattern your life after him? If someone were to ask him to describe you, what would he say about you? Would his description of you be correct? Why?

THE WORLD'S VIEW OF MASCULINITY

Whew. This is a lot to think about, isn't it? There is a definition of masculinity that you are acquainted with. It is a popular definition. In fact, we can guarantee that you have tried to become a man in this way. Don and I have tried this way, also, and failed. Let's look at the three major points:

1. Athletic Ability: Our culture rewards the athlete. You know what we're saying is true. If you can swish three-pointers, slam dunk like you-

know-who, hit a baseball out of the park in the ninth inning, or dance your way into the end zone with three seconds left on the clock, you are treated like a god. You are invited to all the cool parties to hang with all the cool people. You're the man.

2. Sexual Conquest: As an athlete you attract beautiful women. You move from the field or the court to the bedroom. Your ability to reduce the virgin population of the 'hood reveals your manhood. Having a pretty woman on your arm further enhances your image as a man's man in everybody's eyes.

3. Economic Success: What kind of car do you drive? What kind of house do you live in? How much money do you make? People notice these things. Having the cash to make things happen is the final piece of the puzzle. It puts the image of masculinity together.

When you put these three things together, the world wants to elevate you to dizzying heights. Having worked closely with professional athletes since 1979, I (Joel) can tell you that the average guy at the pro level enjoys all three parts of the world's definition of manhood. They seem to have it made. But, it is lonely. Their position in life attracts a lot of insincere people.

JOE EHRMANN'S WAKE UP CALL

Former NFL Baltimore Colts great, Joe Ehrmann, is reflective. He has experienced the intoxicating power of pro athletics. He's been there. A former party animal, he blew his knees out during his football years. So these days he can be seen as a hulk of a man in his mid 40s, hobbling around with a cane. Not a pretty sight.

His dad was a pro boxer. His dad drilled his idea of masculinity into Joe in the basement of their home. Joe would put the gloves on, and his dad would deliberately out-box him, shaming him. The lesson was: "Men don't cry. Men don't need. Real men know how to dominate." This theme was almost literally pounded into his head.

High school football was a life or death struggle for Joe to show his father that he had become a man. He achieved on the field. The scouts noticed. Next thing Joe knew he was in the NFL. But when he got to the big league, he suffered from what we have referred to earlier as Destination Sickness.

He had pro football, women, and money. He had finally arrived to what he thought was manhood only to discover that the empty hole inside his heart was still there. He had changed his environment, but he had brought his same old self and his pain to the new arena.

As a young warrior, driven by rage, he was still trying to live his life for his father. It was crazy. His dad was still not satisfied. In fact, as Joe looked around the NFL at the players, he saw other warriors driven by rage. Few of his friends, he discovered, had good relationships with their fathers. It hit him hard. Here he was in the NFL, at the pinnacle of success, playing with a bunch of guys who weren't in touch with the real internal drive behind their success: Rage. And some of these guys thrived on being over the edge in everything they did—spending money, dealing with women, you name it.

He started taking drugs to medicate the pain and to try to fill up the hole in his heart. He lost perspective, going over the edge with the rest. All of a sudden, he was confronted with an impossible situation that jerked his chain real hard. His brother died. This drew him up short. Reality check! "All that I invested my masculinity in couldn't answer this question. . . . What is the purpose of life?"

It wasn't long before Joe asked the Master Warrior, Jesus, to guide his life. Things began to change. One of the things that was directly affected was his view of masculinity. After the years in pro football, his hunger for God's Word had increased so much that he enrolled in seminary to study the Bible.

Joe says that we all need a father figure, a mentor. This person keeps refocusing us on Jesus. There are so many good things that can pull us off the track. An older, wiser man can see things we can't see. This gentle accountability keeps us on the straight and narrow. Even Jesus would leave the disciples and all the activity to hear words of affirmation from His Father, "This is My beloved Son in Whom I am well pleased."

Joe also believes that each of us needs a brother. The average man has many acquaintances, but not one true, face-to-face friend—one who will tell you the truth when you mess up and still love you.

Joe has a passion for young men to understand that it is not wrong to possess athletic abilities, to be admired by women, or to desire to make tons of money. The real rub comes when we expend the bulk of our energy trying to find meaning in things that won't matter 1,000 years from now.

The world has already defined masculinity. God demands nothing but the best. And He gives us the power to be all He wants us to be. But He won't force us.

Joe has learned a lot. Having suffered much, he has learned to understand the language of pain endured by others. A man of excellent character, he has started an urban outreach in Baltimore and is a champion for racial conciliation. He believes that true manhood is the number one crisis in America. I agree. So many social problems can be dealt with if we as men will yield to the Master Warrior, Jesus.

Christianity to many black men appears feminine. Leon, a man on the street, told me, "Church is for young kids and women. As soon as I got big enough, I pulled out of church. I've been around enough to see the hypocrisy of the leaders and the foolish behavior of the members. I don't see anything in church that can hold my interest on a Sunday morning. That's just the way it is." He then raised his hand and began to mimic and mock the sing-song style of preaching, "I tell you brothers and sisters, that. . . ."

Muslims have painted their own picture of masculinity. In fact, part of the appeal of the Muslims in urban America is the combination of a demanding religion with a "macho" persona. In Newsweek, Carla Power and Allison Samuels write:

> *Most important, Islam's emphasis on dignity and self-discipline appeals to many men in the inner city, where disorder prevails. Muslims are expected to pray five times a day, avoid drugs and alcohol and take care of their families. "Even the manner of walking is different," says Ghayth Nur Kashif, imam of a mosque in southeast Washington. When young men are first introduced to Islam, he says, many come in strutting—"swaying from side to side or walking with a limp. In very short order the limp and swinging stops."[1]*

Men are looking for something they can give their lives to. This is evidenced by the number of men who responded to the Million Man March in October, 1995. Most weren't there because they believed in Louis Farrakhan. They came because of a hunger to be men who are leaders—positive role models.

BISHOP PHIL PORTER PACKS A POWERFUL PUNCH

Ever hear of Promise Keepers? Started by a football coach in Colorado, thousands upon thousands of men from all races flock to sports stadiums and arenas across the country each year to renew their commitment to Christ, to integrity, sexual purity, family, friends, church, racial reconciliation, and to the world. It is a powerful experience!

Bishop Phil Porter, chairman of the board of Promise Keepers, has a passion for young African American males to grasp that the most important way we understand our masculinity is by falling in love with the Person of Jesus Christ and to never allow our hearts to grow cold toward Him.

Phil grew up in a preacher's home on the rough side of the tracks in Enid, Oklahoma. At age 9, he went forward to receive Jesus as his personal Savior. His parents were strict, and the other kids picked on him. "Hey, why don't you take a puff on this cigarette? Mmmm, this beer is good, preacher boy."

At 13, a guy went too far and Phil hit him, knocking him out cold. It felt so good that he started training at the local gym to become a boxer. At 14, he became a terror, searching for those who used to pick on him. If they wouldn't fight, he'd run them down and beat them up anyway. He got so much satisfaction out of all this that he turned semi-pro. He even got paid! By the bullet-proof age of 19, he had won 49 out of 53 bouts.

One night he met his match, a switching southpaw. The guy cold-cocked him. Phil hit the canvas for the first time. God had his attention that evening, but Phil was not a quitter. In his heart he wanted to continue to fight. But God let him know in no uncertain terms what he was to do. He felt a strong tug toward the ministry. After much deliberation he decided to lay down his gloves and become a warrior in the pulpit. Phil had finally met his match. And his arms were too short to box with God!

If Phil were talking with you right now, he wouldn't be handing you a formula, "10 Steps to Become a Man's Man." Instead he would be telling you about The Man, Jesus. Listen to him.

> *Fall in love with Jesus. Fall in love with His Word. Spend time with Him in prayer. Dare to follow Him, and He will guide you with regard to the specifics of life. He will help you to open up with your dad, or help you find*

a man who can be like a father to you. He will help you choose your friends. He will help you to grasp the importance of church participation. He will guide you as you struggle with sexual impurity. He will show you how to give back to your community. He will give you a personal vision, a cause that is bigger than you are.

Bishop Porter says that Jesus is offering you a vision that is bigger than you are. Do you have the courage to accept it? This is a call to young warriors who realize that the road is tough, sometimes unfair, but who are willing to follow the Master Warrior into any battle. We'll catch a glimpse of the vision Jesus may be handing you. But just before we do, let's look at something disturbing.

Time Out

1. In your own words describe your view of masculinity. How does that perspective fit into real life on the street? How does it fit into what the Bible teaches about masculinity?

2. Do you regularly attend church? Why? What is your idea of a good Christian?

3. Explain what it means to fall in love with Jesus.

4. What is your understanding of Islam? How does that fit into the teachings of the Bible?

5. Are your arms too short to box with God? How do you know?

21 | Doing Violence to the Victim

We live in a violent world. Watch the news. . . . "Film at 11." Check out the latest hit movie. Listen to the bullets whizzing down the street, ricocheting off the walls. Black on black crime. Violence is everywhere. Art imitates life. Life imitates art.

Look at the swinging elbows and crunching bodies of basketball players as several men go up for a rebound at the same time. What about football? Observe how savagely the ball carrier gets tackled to the ground. Where else do you find guys so big who can move so fast? Football collisions are violent and spectacular. In *A Thinking Man's Guide to Pro Football*, the author talks in plain language about what kind of impact is experienced when two football players collide at full speed.[1]

Imagine yourself at a Washington Redskins versus Dallas Cowboys game. You have great seats on the 50-yard line. The ball is snapped . . . the quarterback hands off to his running back . . . he makes a break . . . wham! Incredible! A 250-pound lineman capable of running forty yards in 5.0 seconds collides with the 200-pound running back, capable of scampering forty yards in just 4.6 seconds. The crowd is on its feet. The players stagger around for a few moments.

People who are smarter than I have figured out something surprising. The resultant kinetic energy from the collision of these two men produces enough force to move a stack of 66 half-ton pickup trucks (33 tons) one inch! The impact experienced is 1,000 times the force of gravity! No wonder ex-NFLer, Joe Ehrmann, is walking around with a cane.

ASSAULT AND BATTERY OF A DIFFERENT NATURE

Let's leave the football field and capture a glimpse of the assault and battery our Master Warrior, Jesus, experienced during the final hours of His earthly ministry. The punishment those football players endured is nothing when compared to the violence done to this Victim. I was first introduced to the extreme manner of Jesus' suffering while reading something written by a medical doctor. Dr. Truman Davis was deeply touched by the crucifixion of Jesus as he viewed what happened from a medical perspective. As you read, keep in mind that Jesus was an innocent victim who can relate to what your ancestors endured under the cruelty of many slavemasters. Jesus would have endured this violence even if you were the only person on the planet. He loves you this much.

> In the early morning Jesus, battered and bruised, dehydrated (suffered loss of water), and exhausted from a sleepless night, is taken across Jerusalem to the praetorian (guard) of the Fortress Antonia. . . . Preparations for the scourging (whipping) are carried out.

> The prisoner is stripped of His clothing and His hands are tied to a post above His head. A Roman legionnaire (soldier) steps forward with a flagrum (whip) in his hand. This is a short whip consisting of several heavy leather thongs with two small balls of lead attached near the end of each. The heavy whip is brought down with full force again and again across Jesus' shoulders, back and legs.

> At first the heavy thongs cut through the skin only. Then, as the blows continue, they cut deeper into the subcutaneous tissues (found beneath the skin), producing first an oozing of blood from the capillaries (tiny blood vessels) and veins of the skin, and finally spurting bleeding from arterial (larger) blood vessels in the underlying muscles. . . .

> Finally, the skin of the back is hanging in long ribbons; and the entire area is an unrecognizable mass of torn, bleeding tissue. When it is determined by the army captain in charge that the prisoner is near death, the beating is finally stopped.[2]

In this book we have already talked a little about the prophet Isaiah. The ancient prophet declared that the Master Warrior would endure such violence to His face and body that people would be shocked and cover their eyes at the mere sight of Him. Isaiah also had said that His appearance would be so changed that you could barely tell He was human.

How is it that His face would be so damaged—more than any man? I discovered the answer when reading Mark's description of the suffering Savior: Some of the people there spit at Jesus. They covered his eyes and hit him with their fists. They said, "Prove that you are a prophet!" Then the guards led Jesus away and beat him (Mark 14:65 CEV). Two words leaped out at me when I read this verse: "Hit" and "beat". I have a book that tells me what the readers of these words would have understood about them some 2,000 years ago.

"Hit"[3] indicates that someone is hammered repeatedly with clenched fists. The specific target of those knock-out punches is the face, where the blows quickly raise huge welts. Any normal man would die of a cerebral hemorrhage, football players included.

The second term that indicates the violence done to this innocent man is "beat".[4] This word indicates a series of blows. Some think that He was battered with rods rather than with the palms of hands. The physical trauma intensified when the heavy 90-pound beam of the cross was tied across His shoulders. The weight of the wooden beam, combined with extreme blood loss, pushed Him beyond human endurance. We cannot even imagine the pain He must have experienced as the rough wood gouged into the lacerated skin and muscles of His shoulders.

It was sin—your sin, my sin—that compelled Jesus to suffer such violence to His body and mind. This is how much He hated sin. This is how committed He was and is to you and me! Our sin (whether it be sex outside of marriage, drugs, gang-banging, racism, or personal indifference to the violence done to this Victim) separates us from fellowship with our Master Warrior. When we sin, it's like we are right there with the cruel guards and soldiers, smashing Him in the face.

And His response? "Father forgive them because they don't fully know what they are doing." He loves us, not because of our love of and appreciation for Him or for what He has done. Nor does He love us because of our obedience. He loves us—just because. We'll never be able to figure it all out, this side of heaven.

Jesus is painfully aware of the victimization your forefathers endured. In the *Narrative of the Life of Frederick Douglass,* we are reminded of the results. When Frederick was about 16 years old, his owner leased him to Mr. Covey for a year. Listen carefully to the effects of violence.

> Mr. Covey succeeded in breaking me. I was broken in body, soul, and
> spirit. My natural elasticity was crushed, my intellect languished, the dis-

position to read departed, the cheerful spark that lingered about my eye died; the dark night of slavery closed in upon me; and behold a man transformed into a brute!5

Jesus has bottled every teardrop ever shed over these injustices. Real pain demands real answers. When we meet Him in eternity, He will give us those answers yet hidden from our minds. When we see Him, we'll understand all the "whys". We are all—black and white—still affected by the history of slavery in this country. The psyche of slavery is still deeply embedded in all of us. That subtle legacy cannot change until we recognize our own darkness of heart and mind and are willing to expose it to the glorious light and love of Jesus Christ. Our daily challenge is to do just that. This is true masculinity!

Time Out

1. Reread Dr. Davis' medical view of what Jesus suffered. Try to describe it in your own words to a younger brother or sister or friend.

2. Try an experiment. For the next seven days, whenever you pray, just ask God to reveal to you how much He loves you. Nothing else.

3. How does what Jesus endured relate to what your forefathers experienced at the hands of slavemasters? What positive purpose could have possibly come out of it all? Anything?

4. If you are not of African descent, reread Frederick Douglass' words, trying to grasp the dehumanizing effects of slavery and domination.

22 | Fields "Black" for Harvest

H uh? What's this all about? Fields that are "black" for harvest? I'll explain in a few pages. I know, it's a bit corny—a play on Jesus' words when He said to His disciples, "Lift up your eyes and look at the fields for they are already 'white' for harvest."

But stick with me. We are about to take a turn in the road. Wait a minute! I see the faint glow of glory off in the distance! Can you see it?

We (Don and I) are thrilled that you have stuck with us on this "return to glory." We have taken quite a trip together, both inward and upward. Now we're ready for the outward journey.

GOOD COMES OUT OF EVIL

Remember Joseph? As a young man he had a dream that, when it was revealed, made him the object of intense hatred and violence from his older brothers.

You can imagine him huddling in the bottom of an empty pit in the wilderness or stumbling along as a purchased slave in the dust of an Ishmaelite camel on its way to the slave market in Egypt, all the while wondering if maybe he had improperly interpreted the dream about twelve sheaves in the field, the sun, the moon, and eleven stars. Maybe it didn't mean that his family would bow down to him after all. Maybe the dreams were only hallucinations.

To make matters worse, some time after his arrival in Egypt he was framed by his new master's wife. When Joseph refused to be sexually seduced by her, it looked like he was going to do "throw-away-the-key-life-sentence-without-parole" prison duty (read Genesis 37-50).

But, hey, we've read the whole story and we can see the bigger picture. Before all was said and done, Joseph became governor over all the land of Egypt and was used mightily by God to help thousands of people survive during a severe famine. Years passed and his dream was fulfilled. Joseph could then proclaim to his brothers, "You plotted evil against me, but God turned it into good in order to preserve the lives of many people who are alive today because of what happened" (see Genesis 50:20).

AN ANCIENT STORY WITH MODERN APPLICATION

God promotes prepared people. Look at all the heartache and pain Joseph had to go through before he experienced the fulfillment of the dream. Like what happened to Joseph, the return to glory is not an easy path. But how does this relate to us right now, here in North America?

Thousands of black men and women with dreams and aspirations were captured and then shipped over to these American shores because of the slave trade. With all we know about the suffering and the horror, it takes a courageous African American with vision to repeat Joseph's words with heart-felt meaning. "Whites plotted evil against us, but God has turned it into good."

Black people were the fountain, the very spring from which civilization as we know it has flowed. Yet, the black man fell from this high pinnacle. Now Isaiah has prophesied a "return to glory." What is it? The glow off in the distance is getting brighter. Can you see it a little more clearly?

RETURN TO GLORY

In spite of all the problems here, North America is the richest land of opportunity in the world. This is not merely an arrogant statement made by an American. This is reality. Any one who has traveled extensively agrees. There is nothing like this place on the planet. That's why people from around the globe dream about the potential of migrating here to American soil.

For some reason known only to God, you were planted in North America. You did not grow up in Africa. This country is what you know. Generations ago, the slave traders meant it for evil. What happened and how it happened was evil. There still is a whole lot of evil going on today!

But God specializes in this kind of stuff. Like what Bishop Phil Porter said a few chapters ago, "Fall in love with Jesus. . . . He will give you a personal vision, a cause that is bigger than you are." Remember?

This personal vision; this cause that is bigger than you are; this return to glory is about missions—building the invisible kingdom of God in the community right where you are. Giving back and investing God's love in the younger generation.

In ancient times, black people built the most awesome civilizations in human history. We're not talking, though, about bricks and mortar here. This book is but a small part of what God is using to call black people around the world to return to glory. To return to leadership, power, and respect within the community.

The powerful stirring begins with black men. Women and children and nations rejoice when men are real men of character, forgiveness, purity, and integrity. Promise keepers. Men of our word. For too long we have been filled with self-hatred, passivity, distrust, selfishness, greed, and envy . . . and excuses. Only Jesus can change the matters of the heart. And He does.

This also is a call to world missions. As we become vision-driven, we are filled with "the God of the impossible." He delights in moving us into new adventures. But do you feel inadequate? Are you imperfect? Do you feel like a failure sometimes?

If you answered "yes" to any of those last questions, you are a prime candidate to be used by God in this manner!

God has given you special abilities. Is it computers? Athletics? Auto repair? Public speaking? Whatever it is, give it back to Him. Tell Jesus that you are willing to go anywhere, to do anything for Him. Be daring. A man of courage. A true warrior fueled only by an eternal purpose.

Go to school to train. Become an expert in your special ability. Then be available to go to another country or stay in your community with your ability and your love for Jesus.

To be honest, most white churches barely have a flicker of desire for foreign or domestic missions. In these days, God is causing a revival to happen within the hearts of young African American men. Young warriors who are totally sold out to Jesus. Do you feel the stirring in your heart?

The new emerging world marketplaces are in the southern regions: Africa, the Caribbean, South America, the Indian subcontinent, southern

Asia. These are places where a white person sticks out like a sore thumb.

Plus many nations in the regions listed are sick and tired of white imperialism. Here's another interesting reality. The "average" gangbanger on the streets of Watts, Harlem, or southeast D.C. has more consumer knowledge than the presidents of some developing nations. These new emerging marketplaces are "black" for harvest.

An African American man who has taken the inward and upward journeys is a priceless gift to people wherever he goes, whether home or abroad. Especially when it is wrapped around a special ability that is meeting the practical needs of other people. And when the skin color matches, it is one less barrier to overcome in the process.

The needs are overwhelming in the inner cities. I don't need to describe the scene. It seems to be hopeless. Socio-economic justice is a very important piece of the puzzle. More government programs aren't the answer. The fields are "black" unto harvest within a mile radius of where you are at this very moment. Let others curse the darkness. But you can light a candle and brighten the corner where you are. Then inspire someone else to do the same.

Spiritual revival can start a dramatic change that will affect the very core of our society. The change begins with you and Don and me . . . yielding our hearts to the Master Warrior, Jesus Christ. He said He would fight our battles. With Him on our side, we can't lose. What will be important twenty years from now? What will matter a thousand years from now? Discover the answers to these questions. Don't let anything stop you. Don't let anyone deter you. Return to glory by keeping the eternal perspective in clear view and by keeping your heart tender toward Jesus. *Carpé diem*—Seize the day!

Time Out

1. Review the Joseph story in Genesis chapters 37, 39-45 (note especially 45:4-8). What about Joseph impacts you the most? Why?

2. God promotes prepared people. What does that mean? How can a person get prepared?

3. What does the return to glory mean to you personally and for black people? Do you sense a stirring in your heart?

4. How can your special abilities be used by God to build His kingdom? How will you know when you are helping Him build His kingdom?

5. Do you think you are ready to yield your life completely to Jesus? Why?

6. Missions. What does that word mean to you?

7. If you are not of African descent, in what way(s) is God tugging at your heart? Will you obey?

Warriors With a Purpose
Hall of Fame

THIS HALL OF FAME WOULD BE COMPLETE IF YOUR NAME WERE HERE.
THERE IS A SPOT RESERVED FOR YOU.

LENNY MOORE, MAN OF HUMILITY

A first-round draft pick, Lenny Moore played twelve years with the Baltimore Colts before retiring in 1967. In 1975, he was inducted into the Pro Football Hall of Fame.

As a program specialist with the Maryland Juvenile Justice Administration, Moore counsels troubled youth and families. The stakes are higher than in any of his gridiron contests. "My focus is on prevention and intervention with regard to behavioral disorders," says Moore. "Some of these kids are just a step away from the penitentiary."

Even so, he believes that "all kids have some potential, and I hope to bring out that positive potential in them." The game is new, but Moore's personal playbook remains the same: the Bible. "Most of what I tell the kids is right out of the Book," he says.

"You can't save the whole world," says Moore. "All you can do is reach out and touch the people you can touch."

GLENN R. PLUMMER, MAN OF COURAGE

"Jesus was not born in Bethlehem of Judea, but in Sandersville, Georgia!" This proclamation by Nation of Islam leader Louis Farrakhan caused a traffic jam in the phone lines of The 700 Club as shocked viewers responded to excerpts of the five-part video series "Farrakhan: Charismatic Beacon or Cult Leader?"

The series was produced by Glenn Plummer, the only African American owner of a Christian television station in the country. The rarely seen video footage reveals Million Man March leader Farrakhan saying, "I'm hanging on the cross right now. And I'm on Calvary, right now. And I'm ready to go all the way. Because I know that by my stripes every one of you will be healed. You don't have to look anywhere for your Jesus. I represent Him!"

The CEO of TV-26 Detroit and TV-61 New Orleans says,

> All of the video footage of Mr. Farrakhan aired during our five-hour special was completely in context. . . . I am convinced that the Christian black community is being seduced and deceived and I feel compelled to inform them of the danger. I am willing to stand up for my Christian convictions regardless of the consequences. I don't challenge Mr. Farrakhan on social or political issues although I may have some disagreements with him in those areas. My issue with him is on theological grounds, because he is saying one thing to his followers in private and another to the black Christian community in public.

DARRELL GREEN, MAN OF COMPASSION

As Number 28, Darrell has brought cheering Redskins fans to their feet for many years in his NFL career as a cornerback. During the 80s God birthed the Darrell Green Youth Life Foundation. Green says it well, "I was working in Washington, D.C., as a recreation guy and the idea for the foundation came. Drive-by shootings were prevalent in the area. Playing marbles in the streets or riding dirt bikes or whatever you used to do after school was a thing of the past. There just might be stray bullets flying down the street.

> "One night, after several months working there, as I drove back to my home in the suburbs from a recreation department-sponsored Christmas party, I started to cry. I guess my heart just became overloaded with what I was seeing—a lot of devastation, children under-dressed for the cold, alcoholism, and so much more. The whole scene was not good. My heart broke.

> I called some lawyers up and developed this foundation. It started out just as food and clothing distribution. From there we created a learning center to provide academic and moral guidance, training these children to not only give respect, but also to command respect through their behavior.

These kids need a future. If we do not help. If the divorce rate and the degradation of the inner cities continue to progress. If no one forms a partnership with these single mothers and fathers or with the school systems or the church, we are not going to be successful as a nation.

I felt like God was saying, "You know, Darrell, you're out there and what you're doing is great, but you may as well go back to the suburbs and don't come back to the inner city. If you do come back to these needy kids, come back with something that is lasting and real."

And Darrell has obeyed.

SPENCER BARTLEY, MAN OF PERSEVERANCE

Spencer Bartley is in much demand these days. He can keep a crowd on the edge of its seats. To hear him speak you would never know that as a child he was a slow learner, was diagnosed as hyperactive, and that he had been plagued with a stuttering problem. He grew up knowing what it was like to be a survivor. Maybe that's what ultimately drew him, as a district training manager for Southland Corporation, to help 522 developmentally disabled youngsters and at-risk young adults to get jobs.

These are special people. With no need to work directly with the customers or deal with the registers, they are called "support clerks." It was March, 1986, when the first graduate from the job training program went to work at a 7-Eleven store. A week later Spencer received a call from the shift supervisor stating, "Mr. Bartley, please come over here as soon as possible. The young man is in the back room and I can't stop him from crying."

Spencer rushed right over. He went to the back room. "What's the problem, son?" The sobbing fellow looked up at him, reached into his pocket and pulled out a piece of paper. "I'm so happy!" he responded. "My first paycheck!" The simplicity of this young man's gratitude hit Spencer right between the eyes. He was hooked from that moment on. He knew that God had given him a special mission in life and nothing was going to stop him.

MELVIN FORBES, MAN WITH EXTRAORDINARY VISION

Melvin Forbes, the 12th child of farming parents, is a man from humble North Carolinian beginnings. "Flash," as they used to call him in high school, had his pro basketball aspirations ruined when he tore all the ligaments in his foot after a bad landing from a crowd-pleasing 360° slam dunk. Through every setback in his life, though, Mel kept his vision for excellence intact. He became an inspiration to many people.

Not long after, a man came to his small town talking about the future opportunity in computers. Mel was intrigued, accepting an offer to learn at a computer school. He was a quick study. At the end of his training he was offered a job at NASA on the Apollo 16 and Apollo 17 projects. Little did he realize that all the experiences in his life would help him to be an inspirational leader against drug abuse.

Prior to joining Corporations Against Drug Abuse (CADA) as President and CEO, he honed his business skills at MCI, Amtrak, GEICO, and the Goddard Space Flight Center. Under his direction, CADA seeks to sustain its leading role in substance abuse prevention by connecting the core competencies of businesses directly to communities in need through a variety of innovative programs. An ounce of prevention is better than a pound of cure.

Whether speaking at the UN, the White House, or in front of a group of elementary school kids, Mel comes back to a three-part recurring theme: RESPECT. RESPONSIBILITY. RESTRAINT.

Mel knows where his vision comes from. "I was born to make a difference and I have given my life to Jesus Christ. I've been blessed with the greatest parents who have ever walked the face of this earth. Also, my brothers and sisters have made a great impact upon my life, especially my brother and spiritual advisor, Bishop L. N. Forbes. The bottom line is that all that I am or ever hope to be I owe it all to God."

JERALD JANUARY, MAN OF INSPIRATION

Growing up in Detroit about six blocks from Rosa Parks' house, Jerald January could have easily been a statistic—his mother gunned down before he reached kindergarten—his neighborhood burned in the riots of 1967. And a suicide attempt at age sixteen.

Then God said, "Try Me first." And when God called, Jerald answered. He found a gospel bigger than his problems, more powerful than racism, and wondrous enough to put his life to use.

For eighteen years he worked in inner-city youth and community ministries along with coaching high school sports. As the USA director for Compassion International and an inspirational and motivational speaker, January has written two exciting books *A Messed-Up Ride or a Dressed-Up Walk* and *A Second Time*.

WELLINGTON BOONE, MAN OF PRAYER

What would you think about the future of a boy conceived out of wedlock by a mother who tried to abort him twice? What if you knew that by the time he was five he was running the streets till midnight? Any hope for this youngster?

As bishop and founder of the Fellowship of International Churches, few speakers excite and inspire audiences like Wellington Boone. With the odds stacked against him, he yielded his life to Jesus as a young man and God has used him mightily. He has spoken to well over a million men about the subjects of personal revival, denominational unity, building strong families, and racial reconciliation. "Our inward change of character will be reflected in our relationships."

Wellington is calling America to prayer. He is calling people to meet with God in the closets of intercession until their lives are changed and they develop godly character, biblical integrity, and unconditional love for all people.

He is launching a nationwide back-to-the-Bible movement to put the Word of God into the hands of people of all walks of life. He is driven by the reality that God can and will bring revival, even in the most desperate inner cities of America.

Bishop Boone says, "My desire is to get the Bible into every home in our inner cities and into the hands of every college student. God will use His Word to awaken the hearts of people who can make a difference in America's greatest areas of need."

FRED HICKMAN, MAN OF TRANSPARENCY

You have probably seen Fred Hickman on CNN Sports Tonight with Nick Charles . . . "the Hick and Nick show." The promos hail them as the "best dressed, best meshed" duo anywhere. They also could be the "most blessed." Both are believers in Jesus. Fred says, "The Christian life for me comes in stages. You grow and then push a little harder to the next step."

Born in 1956 in Abe Lincoln country, Springfield, Illinois, Fred found it easy to perceive himself as "12 feet tall and bullet-proof" at the boy-wonder stage of his television career. At 22, when most other kids are wondering what to do with their lives, Fred was anchoring news-sports-weather on the hometown WICS TV. Two years later he moved up to the big time in Atlanta. He has been through some tough times, but he doesn't look back.

Talking with Fred is refreshing. No "blah-blah-blah" from him. When he tells it like it is, he makes sense. What you see is what you get. When asked about racism he says, "If people don't like me because I'm black, that's their problem. They can't lure me into hating them. I love them anyway!"

His "mustard seed" message to young black men is: "There are many discouraging aspects about this country, this world. We are often portrayed in low terms as thugs, as emotion-driven people in the mass media. Don't buy it. You know better. Go with what you know. Study history. Find out where we are now by seeing where we've come from. Most of all, study the life of Jesus. He is the only One who can give you the answers to your questions: Who am I? Why am I here? Where am I going?"

C. JEFFREY WRIGHT, MAN OF EXCELLENCE

Born in 1954, growing up in northeast Washington, D.C., Jeffrey has gone up against incredible odds and has attained unusual success without disintegrating under the pressure. He and his six brothers had a good foundation. His dad worked as the chosen personal assistant to Supreme Court Chief Justice Earl Warren and then to Justice Warren Burger. His mother worked in the public library system of DC and later headed the library system for the University of the District of Columbia's. Quite the heritage!

Motivated by the desire to do the most with what God gave him, Jeff received a Juris Doctor degree from Georgetown University Law Center. He then completed his MBA in Finance and International Business from Columbia University on the prestigious Johnson & Johnson Leadership Scholarship Award. He had already been promoted to the corporate legal staff of TWA, but after earning his MBA, he was appointed to the position of Vice President, Corporate Development—Consumer Health & Personal Care Groups for Bristol-Myers Squibb. In spite of all this success he knew there was an even higher calling for his life.

In 1995, with all this experience in corporate America, Jeff took over as the president of Chicago-based Urban Ministries, the only independent, African American owned and operated, Christian publishing company producing Sunday School curricula, books, and black Christian video and film. Using the finest possible material, Jeff views this as the greatest opportunity of his career, to be able to impact the lives of thousands of people with the message that Jesus loves them.

Jeff has become a dear friend. In fact after a number of long discussions, his stories, his pain, and his ideas have provided much inspiration for my (Joel) part of this book. Don and I owe him a great debt of gratitude.

Clarence Walker, Man of the Bible

Since you have already read this book, you know that Dr. Clarence Walker's audio packet, "The Princely Proclamation Series: God's Exciting Plan for Black People," was the original inspiration behind much of Don Griffin's part of this book. We owe Clarence a great debt of gratitude. One of the main things you realize when hearing Clarence preach is that this man is serious about biblical scholarship! He doesn't mess around. And he can preach!

Clarence has a Ph. D. in counseling from Trinity Theological Seminary and an M.S.W. from Temple University and is a licensed marriage and family counselor. His books, *Biblical Counseling with African Americans* and *Breaking Strong Holds in the African American Family* (Zondervan), have a wide readership.

Growing up in the tough section of North Philadelphia raised by his grandparents, surrounded by gang warfare, family dysfunction, and racism at every turn, Clarence has not wasted his sorrows. Instead he and his wife, Ja'Ola, have permitted Jesus to borrow them to minister healing to thousands through counseling, seminars, teaching, preaching, drama, and audio/video tapes.

The Admiral, David Robinson

You can tell a lot about what a professional athlete brings to his game by looking at his nickname, especially in basketball. Wilt Chamberlain was "The Stilt," Earvin Johnson, "Magic", and Michael Jordan, "Air".

David Robinson is "The Admiral." David's nickname comes from his days at the U. S. Naval Academy because of his ability to take charge on the court and lead his teammates to victory.

He lived up to his title when he joined the San Antonio Spurs in the 1989-90 season after serving a required two-year stint in the Navy. Some wondered how long it would take the 7 ft. 1 in., 235 lb. center to get his "sea legs" among a fleet of NBA heavyweights. But after he scored 26 points in a 109-92 victory over the New Jersey Nets his rookie year, one of the opposing guards remarked, "If he's still learning the game, I'd hate to see him when he knows it cold."

ALL STAR ADMIRAL

In his seasons with the Spurs, David has shown over and over just how adept he is at "learning the game." He has become one of the dominant centers in pro basketball mainly because of his superb agility and speed. In 1990 he was named Rookie of the Year; in 1991 he was named to the All-NBA defensive first team; in 1992 he was voted NBA defensive player of the year; and in 1993 he had his fourth consecutive All-Star season. On top of all that, he has the distinction of having been named to three Olympic basketball teams, including the 1992 and 1996 "Dream Teams." Salute the Admiral, if you please.

David's success is even more admirable given the fact that he was slow to focus his athletic gifts on basketball in college because of his wide range of interests. He has a background in classical piano, jams on a sax, and can often be found arranging music with friend and teammate Terry Cummings. He golfs and enjoys reading science fiction and says that if he weren't in basketball he would probably be a scientist, a musician, or a baseball player. So it was unusual for a man of David's varied interests to devote himself almost entirely to one thing for a couple of months back in 1991—studying the Bible.

THE ADMIRAL FINDS AN ANCHOR

The Bible? Yes, and David explains why: "In June (of 1991) a minister came and talked with me, and he basically said that I wasn't living a Christian life—I needed to take my Christian life very seriously. I knew I should have been reading the Bible and trying to learn more about the Lord. June 8 was the day I vowed to commit my life to the Lord. When I did that, the Lord blessed me in a great way. He made me turn all my energies into the Bible."

David understood that he—like all persons—needed forgiveness to enter into a relationship with God, and that forgiveness comes through trusting in Jesus Christ as one's Savior. Jesus saves us from our sin—the rebellion that causes us to turn our back on God. That sin keeps us from knowing God and enjoying the forgiveness and eternal life that He longs to give us. In fact our sin earns us only death, for the Bible says, "The wages of sin is death" (Romans 6:23).

But God provided a way to forgive our sin when He sent His Son, Jesus Christ, to die in our place, taking our punishment for us. The Bible also says, "Christ died for sins once for all, the righteous for the unrighteous, to bring you to God" (1 Peter 3:18). Christ not only died for us to prove His love, But He also came back to life three days after He was buried to prove His power over death!

Now instead of trying to earn God's favor by being good or doing good (neither of which are acceptable to a perfect God for salvation), God in His mercy simply wants us to accept the payment that He has provided. The Bible calls that "believing in Christ." "God so loved the world that He gave His one and only Son, that whoever believes in Him shall not perish but have eternal life" (John 3:16).

THE ADMIRAL AND HIS COMMANDER

David Robinson is an NBA All Star, the go-to guy in the final critical minutes of a game, the one who doesn't back down on the court. And he is also a child of the King, Jesus Christ, the Savior to whom every knee will eventually bow in submission and worship. If the Admiral saw the need for an anchor in his life, and if he found the forgiveness, stability, and purpose he needed in Jesus Christ, shouldn't you consider Christ, too?

If you would like to know the forgiveness and eternal life that Christ offers freely to all who will trust Him as Savior, you can express the desire of your heart with this short prayer:

> God, I know I fall short of what you demand, and I know that nothing I can do will ever be enough to pay for my sin. Right now I trust Your Son, Jesus Christ, as the payment for my sin, and accept your free gift of forgiveness and eternal life. Come live in me like You promised, and show me how I can serve You because of all You have done for me. Amen.

> Reprinted by permission of the American Tract Society.

If you said this prayer for the first time, we (Don and Joel) would like to hear from you. Please send a self-addressed, stamped envelope to:

Return to Glory
537 Mantua Pike, Suite 203
Woodbury, NJ 08096

Let us know a bit about yourself, and we will respond with some information that will help you grow in your new life with Jesus.

A Message Especially for White Readers

If you have read this book, you already know that I (Joel) am white. Don is African American. Quick story. I grew up in a small farming community of about 2,000 people in Western Canada with one brother and two sisters. The big issue in that part of North America is racism directed toward Native American Indians.

Racial prejudice and bigotry were not a part of the heritage my parents handed me. In the 60s, when I was growing up, we didn't have television in our home, so my contact with the outside world was remote. My dad, a social studies teacher, kept up with current events. The race riots of the 60s pictured in Time and Newsweek seemed so far away. I never gave it much thought, if any.

At the more-questions-than-answers age of 17 I quit high school, stuck out my thumb and left home with twenty-four bucks in my pocket. It was 1971. Peace. Love. Rock and roll. Long hair. Rebellion. California. Marijuana and hashish. Sleeping beside the road. Shop lifting. Panhandling. Survival.

Through a series of circumstances, I traveled to Maine, attending a church on September 10, 1972. Two other times I had visited the church I was stoned, but this night I wasn't. I had a profound conversion experience that evening, signing up for their evening Bible School the very next day. A 180° change!

I am now a little older and wiser. I have been through my own heartaches. I have had a lot of resumé/obituary-type stuff happen. Chaplain of the Washington Bullets/Wizards since 1979. Pioneered and pastored three growing churches over 18 years. Hold a Ph. D. in counseling. Hosted a regional radio talk show for about 11 years. Have written three other books that are in 12 foreign translation editions and have traveled quite literally around much of the world working with people of many cultures and races. Plain and simple, I have been exposed to a lot of life and feel like a seasoned veteran in many areas.

But let me tell you something. Researching and co-writing this book has become an incredible life-changing exercise. Even though I had always believed that I didn't have a racist bone in my body, I am realizing that I really didn't have a clue as to what people of color deal with on a daily basis in this country. This is my story. Perhaps you could take a moment to reflect upon your own experience in this area.

This book project emerged out of some consulting work I had done at the company where Don Griffin works. Quickly we realized that both of us loved Jesus. Don began to share some of the things he had discovered regarding the history of his people and the prominent role that black people had played in the Bible. He also shared a biblical prophecy that communicated some pretty exciting things that God was going to do with blacks in the future.

Returning home from one of our inspiring discussions, I studied the original Hebrew language of the passages Don had mentioned to me and discovered to my greater excitement that it all checked out exactly as he said. This fired me up. Since I am a lover of truth, I felt that we needed to write a book about this subject together, not knowing exactly how it would take shape. Neither of us was interested in a "black thing" or a "white thing." We wanted a book that would ultimately point people back to the Bible and hopefully would create a hunger to learn more about this important topic. Don started writing about the historical/biblical perspectives. I wanted to hitch-hike off his research and write about what all this information meant for the mental, emotional, and spiritual makeup of African American men.

I began to talk with African American men, telling them about the project, asking pointed questions. Immediately, each one was somewhat suspicious, wanting to know my motivation for writing such a book. After all, I am an extremely white man writing to black men. It's crazy, isn't it?

The more questions I asked the deeper each man would get. I saw how much racism defines the identity of blacks. I felt the suppressed, controlled rage of middle class blacks. I felt the survivor guilt of successful blacks trying to assimilate into white America. I discovered that their problems were as much a matter of psychological self-doubts as they were a matter of politics and economics. I heard that forgiveness for the past is not enough, they want to know if they will be allowed to experience social economic justice as a whole race in America.

CONFESSIONS OF A WHITE MAN

It was a wake up call for me. I began to see things about my life of which I had no conscious awareness. As a white man I am not forced to think about racism. People of color deal with it on a daily basis. Even though I have pastored churches with significant numbers of people of color, I have had to examine my inability to establish deeper friendships with people outside my race. This has troubled me.

I have had to examine my well-meant tip-toeing around some blacks. I have known that many blacks are extremely sensitive to subtle racism. There are the well-intentioned overtures of whites who can easily talk about surface things, but never step over the imaginary "racial boundary line" where genuine relationships grow. I have had to look at my own uncomfortability in this area, not wanting to say something stupid or offend on any level. In the past, this has caused me to pull back. Not any more! Black men and white men who know that they are really loved for who they are—just because—open up. This is nothing new. This cannot happen, however, without dialogue, conversation, communication, reaching out, risking. And that's what this book is all about.

We all—black and white—are still affected by the history of slavery in this country. This is a complex challenge. The psyche of slavery is still deeply embedded in the fabric of our society. And we all—white and black—need to initiate change and establish deeper relationships that cross racial lines.

Who will take the first step toward racial conciliation in your sphere of influence? Regardless of your previous experience, I am encouraging you, my white brothers, to take the first step. Here's a plan of action:

    1. Take another look at what Don wrote regarding the prophecy in Isaiah. Do an in-depth Bible study on that and related Scriptures. See and accept what God says about what He is going to do with people of color in these days.

    2. Go to your local library and check out a whole bunch of

educational videos that give you an understanding of what people of color have dealt with in America and in other parts of the world. Also, be sure to borrow videos on the racism Hispanics, Native Americans, Asians, and others have encountered here in America.

Take a few evenings out of your life to watch these videos. It is worth the investment. Be prepared to be moved by what you're watching. Your life will be forever altered. Here are a few suggestions to get you started: a) Africa: A Voyage of Discovery with Basil Davidson, b) Eyes on the Prize, c) The Promised Land

3. Look at the Bibliography in the rear of this book. Look for a few titles that grab you. Borrow them from your local library and read them. They will open your eyes in ways that videos can't.

4. PRAY. The subtle, subjective legacy of slavery and racism cannot change until we recognize our own darkness of heart and mind and be willing to expose it to the glorious light and love of Jesus Christ. Ask God to give you a love for and a desire to get to know others outside your racial comfort zone. If, in the past, you have tried to reach out but have felt rejected, ask God to heal your heart and to give you a renewed passion for reaching out.

Ask God to reveal racism in your heart, even in its most subtle forms. Take the time to really wrestle with this: Smiling/laughing at the punch line of a racist joke. Judging an entire race on the basis of your experiences with a few people. Lack of desire to educate yourself about the history of other cultures. Mentally discounting the ideas or opinions expressed by people of color. Not speaking up when someone is humiliating another. You get the picture. Racism is sin. Sin can be forgiven.

5. *Return to Glory* is a book that Don and I have provided for you not only to read, but also as a tool for you to use as you seek to open the lines of communication to African Americans. Try an experiment. Purchase an extra copy of this book and give it to your African American neighbor, church member, or co-worker. Tell him, "This book has made an impact on my life. I am giving this to you as a gift. Read it and then let's get together for lunch to discuss it."

Three things are accomplished:

a) Generally speaking, we as men find it hard to talk on a more intimate level. In the above scenario, both men will be able to spin off a common experience—the reading of the same book. This will allow you to talk about something other than sports, the weather, church, or your job. And to talk about something that is extremely important and timely.

b) The gesture of a white man giving this book to an African American is awesome. Even though the reverse could happen, it is my opinion that it is not nearly as effective.

c) This book doesn't leave either man hanging in limbo with just a bunch of historical facts and no place to go with that information. After discussing some hard stuff, we provide a road map for wholeness—mentally, emotionally, and spiritually. You may even want to go through this book with him over a period of weeks, discussing the questions at the end of each chapter.

6. Like marriage, racial conciliation is organic. It can grow and blossom, or it can die on the vine if left unattended. Passivity is its greatest enemy.

Racial conciliation is a process, not a destination. It is a lifelong commitment. As in marriage, you cannot really learn, grow, question, or challenge except within the context of a committed, cross-color relationship that has experienced at least two or three knock-down, drag-out verbal battles where everything within you has wanted to quit and run away. If you haven't been there, perhaps you haven't made as much progress as you may think. This is tough stuff. It's not easy. But it is well worth the personal sacrifice. Don't ever quit! We can either curse the darkness or light a candle.

Light a candle and brighten the corner where you are. Racial reconciliation, at any level, puts a smile on God's face.

7. "Trust in the Lord with all your heart, and lean not on your own understanding; In all your ways acknowledge Him, and He shall direct your paths" (Proverbs 3:5-6).

YOU AND I

We meet as strangers, each carrying a mystery within us. I cannot say who you are.

I may never know you completely.

But I trust that you are a man in your own right, possessed of inherent worth and value that are God's richest treasures.

So, by God's grace, I make this promise to you: I will impose no identities upon you, but will invite you to become who you are in God without shame or fear.

I will hold open a space for you in the world and allow your right to fill it with an authentic vocation. For as long as your search takes, you have my loyalty.

–Author Unknown

Notes

Chapter 1

[1] Pastor Greg Stanton, "Preface," *Historical Christianity African Centered*, by James C. Anyike. Chicago: Popular Truth, Inc., 1995.

Chapter 2

[1] A brief discussion of this point is contained in "Africa, the Beginning," *The Original African Heritage Study Bible*, ed. Cain Hope Felder, Nashville: James C. Winston, 1993, p.106.

[2] Ibid., p. 106.

[3] Ibid.

[4] Charles B. Copher, *Black Biblical Studies: An Anthology of Charles B. Copher: Biblical and Theological Issues on the Black Presence in the Bible.* Chicago: Black Light Fellowship, 1993, p. 23.

[5] Dr. Yosef A. A. ben-Jochannan, *Black Man of the Nile and His Family.* Baltimore: Black Classic Press, 1989, p. 128.

[6] Cheikh Anta Diop, *The African Origin of Civilization: Myth or Reality*, ed. and trans. Mercer Cook. Westport, Conn.: Lawrence Hill & Company, 1974, p. 1.

[7] Martin Bernal, *Black Athena: The Afroasiatic Roots of Classical Civilization*, Vol. I, *The Fabrication of Ancient Greece 1785-1985.* New Brunswick, New Jersey: Rutgers University Press, 1987, p. 17.

[8] Diop, p. 1.

[9] Ibid., p. 1.

[10] Herodotus, *Herodotus*, Vol. I, Books 1-2, trans. A. D. Godley. Cambridge, Mass.: Harvard University Press, first published 1920, revised and reprinted 1990, p. 301.

[11] *The New Bible Dictionary*, 2nd ed. Downers Grove, Illinois: InterVarsity Press, 1996, p. 355.

[12] Herodotus, p. 345.

[13] Diop, p. 1.

[14] Diodorus of Sicily, *The Library of History Books*, ii.35-iv.58, trans.

C. H. Oldfather. Cambridge, Mass.: Harvard University Press, first published 1935, reprinted 1994, pp. 93, 95.

[15] Diop, p. 2. Diop draws the obvious conclusion that the Colchians, Egyptians, and Ethiopians were thought by the ancients to be of the same race. This is clear enough for anyone to see, including a "non-scholar".

[16] Dr. Yosef A. A. ben-Jochannan, *Black Man of the Nile and His Family.* Baltimore: Black Classic Press, 1989, p. 179. The fact that ancient writers almost unanimously testify to the blackness of Egyptians is not disputed by scholars.

[17] Ibid.

[18] Gaston Maspero, *The Dawn of Civilization.* London: 1894; reprinted, New York: Frederick Ungar, 1968.

CHAPTER 3

[1] Cheikh Anta Diop, *The African Origin of Civilization: Myth or Reality,* trans. Mercer Cook. Westport, Conn.: Lawrence Hill & Company, 1974, p. 27.

[2] Ibid., pp. 27-28.

[3] Baron Viviant Denon, *Travels in Upper and Lower Egypt,* trans. Arthur Aikin, 3 Vols. New York: p. 1803.

[4] Dr. Yosef A. A. ben-Jochannan, *Black Man of the Nile.* Baltimore: Black Classic Press, 1989, p. 109.

[5] Ibid., p. 194.

[6] Ibid. Credit Baron Vivian Denon with this account. He was an eyewitness. For further discussion, see Dr. Yosef A. A. ben-Jochannan, *Africa: Mother of Western Civilization.* Baltimore: Black Classic Press, 1988, pp. 7-8.

[7] Joseph McCabe, "Life Among the May Peoples of the Earth," p, 26, quoted in John G. Jackson, *Introduction to African Civilizations.* Secaucus, New Jersey: The Citadel Press, 1970, p. 78.

[8] ben-Jochannan, p. 34.

[9] Diop, p. 20.

[10] George Arthur Buttrick, et al, eds. *The Interpreter's Dictionary of the Bible,* vol. 2. Nashville: Abington, 1981, p. 44.

[11] Ibid., p. 44.

[12] Ibid.

[13] Ibid.

[14] Ibid.

[15] Ibid.

[16] ben-Jochannan, p. 230.

[17] Ibid.

[18] Ibid.

[19] Ibid., p. 231.

CHAPTER 4

[1] Cheikh Anta Diop, *The African Origin of Civilization: Myth or Reality,* ed. and tran. Mercer Cook. Westport, Conn.: Lawrence Hill & Company, 1974, p. 253.

[2] Brian Tierney and Sidney Painter, *Western Europe in the Middle Ages.* New York: Alfred A. Knopf, 1974. The authors, in this work, define the Middle Ages as a historical period lasting from 300-1475

[3] Father Clarence Williams, exec. producer, "Search: The Black People's Presence in the Bible," (video transcript). Detroit: Search, 1987, p. 7.

[4] Rev. Walter Arthur McCray, *The Black Presence in the Bible: Discovering the Black and African Identity of Biblical Persons and Nations,* Teachers Guide. Vol. 1. Chicago: Black Light Fellowship, p. 5. The infallibility of the Bible is the position taken by Rev. McCray in this work. We couldn't agree more.

[5] Ibid., p. 20.

[6] Ibid.

[7] Dr. Tony Evans, *Let's Get to Know Each Other.* Nashville: Thomas Nelson, 1995, p. 28.

[8] McCray, p. 20.

[9] Brown, Driver, and Briggs, *A Hebrew-English Lexicon of the Old Testament.* London: Oxford University Press, 1968, p. 871.

[10] *The New Bible Dictionary,* 2nd edition, Downers Grove, Illinois: Inter-Varsity Press, 1996, p. 934. See also George Arthur Buttrick, et al, eds. *The Interpreter's Dictionary of the Bible.* Nashville: Abington, 1981, p. 799.

[11] McCray, p. 20.

[12] Ibid., p. 21.

[13] Ibid.

[14] Frank M. Snowden, Jr., *Before Color Prejudice.* Cambridge, Mass.: Harvard University Press, 1994, p. 73.

[15] McCray, p. 33.

[16] Frank M. Snowden, Jr., *Blacks In Antiquity.* Cambridge, Mass.: The Belknap Press of Harvard University Press, 1970, pp. 198-199, 331.

[17] McCray, p. 32. This is another example used by McCray in his treatment of black presence in the Bible. The prophet here makes a statement of fact. There was no color prejudice exhibited by the biblical writers.

[18] Rev. Walter Arthur McCray, *The Black Presence in the Bible and the Table of Nations Genesis 10:1-32: With Emphasis on the Hamitic Genealogical Line from a Black Perspective, Vol. 2, Table of Nations.* Chicago: Black Light Fellowship, 1994, p. 15.

[19] Ibid., p. 14.

[20] Ibid., p. 15.

[21] Ibid.

CHAPTER 5

[1] Dr. Clarence Walker, "Biblical Prophecy," a sermon on tape. Philadelphia: Clarence Walker Ministries, n.d.

[2] Ibid.

[3] Ibid. Dr. Walker goes into a much more detailed account of the migrations of Jews after the destruction of the Jewish Temple in 70 AD.

[4] Cain Hope Felder, Ph. D., ed., "Africa, The Beginning," *The Original African Heritage Study Bible.* Nashville: James C. Winston, 1993, p. 101.

[5] Ibid., p. 101.

[6] Ibid., p. 102.

[7] Ibid.

[8] John A. Martin, "Isaiah," *The Bible Knowledge Commentary.* John F. Walvoord and Roy B. Zuck, eds. Wheaton, Illinois: Victor Books, 1985, p. 1065.

[9] Ibid.

[10] George Steindorf and Keith C. Seele, *When Egypt Ruled the East.* Chicago: The University of Chicago Press, 1957, p. 271.

[11] Charles B. Copher, "Biblical and Theological Issues on the Black Presence in the Bible," *Black Biblical Studies, An Anthology of Charles B. Copher.* Chicago: Black Light Fellowship, 1993, p. 31. See also *Personalities of Antiquity.* New York: H. W. Wilson, 1932, p. 186.

[12] Chancellor Williams, *The Destruction of Black Civilization: Great Issues of a Race From 4500 B. C. to 2000 A. D.* Chicago: Third World Press, 1987, p. 114.

[13] Dr. Walker exposes this phenomenon in his sermon "Biblical Prophecy."

[14] Ibid.

[15] Ibid. See also James Strong, "Dictionary of the Words in the Hebrew Bible. . . ." *The Complete Word Study Old Testament.* Iowa Falls, Iowa: World, 1994, p. 74.

[16] Ibid. Dr. Walker explains the inappropriateness of the "scattered" translation.

[17] James Strong, "Dictionary of the Words in the Hebrew Bible. . .," *The Complete Word Study Old Testament.* Iowa Falls, Iowa: World, p. 72.

[18] Ibid., p. 72.

[19] Walker.

[20] Ibid.

[21] Ibid. Dr. Walker highlights the youthfulness of the skin of older African Americans to make a current application of the Hebrew word marat. This is a commonly noted trait in the African American community.

[22] Matthew Henry, *Commentary on the Whole Bible.* ed. Leslie F. Church, Ph. D., F. R. Hist. Grand Rapids: Zondervan, 1979, p. 853.

[23] Bishop Alfred G. Dunston, Jr,. *The Black Man in the Old Testament and Its World.* Trenton, New Jersey: Africa World Press, 1992, p. 4.

CHAPTER 6

[1] Dr. Tony Evans, *Let's Get to Know Each Other.* Nashville, Tennessee: Thomas Nelson, 1995, p. 30.

[2] Ibid., p. 30.

[3] William Dwight McKissic, Sr., *Beyond Roots: In Search of Blacks in the Bible.* Wenonah, New Jersey: Renaissance Productions, 1990, p. 16.

[4] Ibid., p. 16.

[5] Ibid., p. 16.

[6] Ibid., p. 16.

[7] Ibid., p. 16.

[8] Ibid., p. 16.

[9] Ibid., p. 20.

[10] Ibid., p. 20.

[11] Ibid., p. 20.

[12] Ibid., p. 20.

[13] Rev. Walter Arthur McCray, *The Black Presence in the Bible and the Table of Nations Genesis 10:1-32: With Emphasis on the Hamitic Genealogical Line from a Black Perspective, Vol. 2, Table of Nations.* Chicago: Black Light Fellowship, 1994, p. 81.

[14] Ibid., p. 82

[15] Ibid.

[16] Ibid.

[17] McKissic, p. 26.

[18] William Dwight McKissic, Sr., and Anthony T. Evans, *Beyond Roots II: If Anybody Ask (sic.) You Who I Am.* Wenonah, New Jersey: Renaissance Productions, 1994, p. 113.

[19] Rev. Walter Arthur McCray, *The Black Presence in the Bible: Discovering the Black and African Identity of Biblical Persons and Nations,* Teachers Guide. Vol. 1. Chicago: Black Light Fellowship, p. 69.

[20] Cain Hope Felder, Ph. D., ed., "Africa's Service To The World," *The Original African Heritage Study Bible.* Nashville: James C. Winston, 1993, p. 111.

[21] Ibid., p. 111.

[22] Ibid.

[23] Ibid.

[24] Ibid.

[25] Ibid.

[26] McCray, Vol. 1, p. 70.

[27] Ibid., p. 9. See also Cheikh Anta Diop, "Origin of the Ancient Egyptians," *General History of Africa: Ancient Civilizations of Africa,* Vol. 2, ed. G. Mokhtar. Berkeley, Calif.: University of California Press, UNESCO, 1981, p. 27.

[28] McKissic, p. 27.

[29] Ibid.

[30] Ibid., p. 27. See also Arthur C. Custance, *Noah's Three Sons: Human History in Three Dimensions,* Vol. 1: *The Doorway Papers,* Grand Rapids: Zondervan, 1975, pp. 98, 151.

[31] Ibid., pp. 27, 28. See also Runoko Rashidi, "More Light on Sumer, Elam, and India," in Ivan Van Sertima and Runoko Rashidi, eds. *African Presence in Early Asia.* New Brunswick, New Jersey: Transaction Books, 1988, p. 163.

[32] Chancellor Williams, *The Destruction of Black Civilization: Great Issues of a Race From 4500 B. C. to 2000 A. D.,* Part I, title P. Chicago: Third World Press, 1987.

[33] Cheikh Anta Diop presents a cogent argument showing that Indo-Europeans never created a civilization in their original homeland. Why? See particularly his discussion in *The African Origin of Civilization: Myth or Reality,* ed. and tran. Mercer Cook. Westport, Conn.: Lawrence Hill & Company, 1974, pp. 151-153.

[34] *The Interpreter's Dictionary of the Bible,* ed. George Arthur Buttrick, et al. Nashville, Tennessee: Abington, 1981, Vol. IV, p. 460.

[35] Ibid.

[36] Ibid., p. 462.

[37] Ibid., pp. 457, 459.

[38] Ibid., p. 457.

[39] Ibid.

[40] Ibid., p. 461.

[41] William Dwight McKissic, Sr., and Anthony T. Evans, *Beyond Roots II: If Anybody Ask (sic.) You Who I Am.* Wenonah, New Jersey: Renaissance Productions, 1994, p. 120.

[42] Strabo, *Geography,* books 15-16, tran. Horace Leonard Jones, ed. G. P. Goold. Cambridge, Mass.: Harvard University Press, first published 1930, reprinted 1995, p. 195.

[43] This view is fully supported and documented in research done by Cheikh Anta Diop. See particularly his discussion in Diop, op. cit., Chapter 5, pp. 100-128.

[44] Diop, pp. 101, 107-123.

[45] Buttrick, p. 463.

[46] Ibid.

47 Ibid.

48 Ibid.

49 Ibid.

50 Allen P. Ross. "Genesis," *The Bible Knowledge Commentary,* ed. John F. Walvoord and Roy B. Zuck. Wheaton, Illinois: Victor Books, p. 44.

51 Ibid., p. 45.

52 Chancellor Williams fully discusses this problem in black society in his most popular work, *The Destruction of Black Civilization.* See his discussion in Williams, op. cit., chapter 12, pp. 298-307.

53 Ross, p. 45.

54 Ibid., p. 45.

55 Ibid.

56 Ibid.

57 Henry M. Morris, *The Genesis Record.* Grand Rapids: Baker, 1976, p. 77.

58 Ibid., p. 77.

59 McKissic and Evans, p. 121.

CHAPTER 7

1 Matthew Henry, *Commentary on the Whole Bible.* ed. Leslie F. Church, Ph. D., F. R. Hist. Grand Rapids: Zondervan, 1979, p. 853.

2 Ibid., p. 853.

3 Ibid.

4 Dr. Clarence Walker preaches on the significance of the name, "Lord of Hosts." The picture of God as a "warrior" taking matters into His own hands and challenging the devil to "make My day" is colorfully painted in one of his sermons. See particularly "Biblical Prophecy," a sermon on tape. Philadelphia: Clarence Walker Ministries, n.d.

5 Henry, p. 853.

6 John A. Martin, "Isaiah," *The Bible Knowledge Commentary,* John F. Walvoord and Roy B. Zuck, eds. Wheaton, Illinois: Victor Books, p. 1033.

7 Ibid., p. 1065.

8 Chancellor Williams, *The Destruction of Black Civilization: Great Issues of a Race From 4500 B. C. to 2000 A. D.* Chicago: Third World

Press, 1987, p. 115.

[9] Ibid., p. 115.

[10] Ibid., p. 117.

[11] Ibid.

[12] Ibid., p. 40.

[13] Dr. Tony Evans, *Let's Get to Know Each Other.* Nashville: Thomas Nelson, p. 33.

[14] Ibid., p. 29. See also *The Interpreter's Dictionary of the Bible.* George Arthur Buttrick, et al, eds. Nashville: Abington, 1981, Vol. III, p. 799.

[15] Cain Hope Felder, Ph. D., ed., "Africa's Service to the World," *The Original African Heritage Study Bible.* Nashville: James C. Winston, 1993, p. 112.

[16] John Dawson, *Healing America's Wounds.* Ventura, Calif.: Regal, 1994, pp. 61-72. An entire discussion of the Civil War and God's judgment on America is taken up by Dawson.

CHAPTER 8

[1] Dr. Clarence Walker, "Biblical Prophecy," a sermon on tape. Philadelphia: Clarence Walker Ministries. n.d.

[2] Ibid.

[3] Chancellor Williams, *The Destruction of Black Civilization.* Chicago: Third World Press, 1987, p. 114. .

[4] Ibid., p. 114.

[5] Ibid.

[6] Ibid., p. 115.

[7] Ibid.

[8] Cheikh Anta Diop. *The African Origin of Civilization: Myth or Reality,* ed. and tran. Mercer Cook. Westport, Conn.: Lawrence Hill & Company, 1974, p. 220.

[9] Ibid., p. 220.

[10] Williams, p. 117.

[11] Diop, p. 221.

[12] Walker.

[13] J. C. deGraff-Johnson, *African Glory: The Story of Vanished Negro Civilizations.* Baltimore: Black Classic Press, 1986, p. 164.

[14] Ibid., p. 164.

[15] Ibid.

[16] Ibid., p. 165.

[17] Ibid.

[18] Ibid., p. 164.

[19] Walker.

[20] Cain Hope Felder, Ph. D., ed. "The Ancient Black Christians," *The Original African Heritage Study Bible.* Nashville: James C. Winston, 1993, p. 1822.

[21] Ibid., p. 1823.

[22] Ibid.

[23] Ibid., p. 1824.

[24] Ibid., pp. 1824, 1825.

[25] Ibid., p. 1825.

[26] Williams, pp. 152-153

[27] Williams, pp. 151-152.

[28] Williams, pp. 151-155, 337.

[29] Walker.

[30] Ibid.

[31] Ibid.

[32] Ibid.

[33] Ibid.

[34] Ibid.

[35] Ibid.

[36] Ibid.

[37] Dr. Tony Evans, *Let's Get To Know Each Other.* Nashville: Thomas Nelson, 1995, p. 95.

[38] Ibid., p. 95.

[39] Ibid.

[40] Ibid., p. 96.

[41] Ibid.

[42] Ibid., p. 98.

[43] Ibid.

CHAPTER 9

[1] Chancellor Williams, *The Destruction of Black Civilization: Great*

Issues of a Race From 4500 B. C. to 2000 A. D. Chicago: Third World Press, 1987, p. 303.

[2] Dr. Tony Evans, *Let's Get To Know Each Other.* Nashville: Thomas Nelson, p. 16.

[3] Dr. Clarence Walker, "Biblical Prophecy," a sermon on tape. Philadelphia: Clarence Walker Ministries, n.d.

[4] Ibid. Walker's characterization of the plight of black people as Satan's field day is very appropriate.

[5] Ibid.

[6] Ibid. See also James Strong, "Dictionary of the Words in the Hebrew Bible. . . ," *The Complete Word Study Old Testament,* Iowa Falls, Iowa: World, 1994, p. 44.

[7] *The New Merriam-Webster Dictionary.* Springfield, Massachusetts: Merriam-Webster, Inc., 1989, p. 621.

[8] Charles B. Copher, "Biblical and Theological Issues on the Black Presence in the Bible," *Black Biblical Studies, An Anthology of Charles B. Copher.* Chicago: Black Light Fellowship, 1993, p. 23.

[9] Ibid., p. 23.

[10] Ibid.

[11] Cheikh Anta Diop. *The African Origin of Civilization: Myth or Reality,* ed. and tran. Mercer Cook. Westport, Conn.: Lawrence Hill & Company, 1974, p. 45.

[12] Ibid., p. 45.

[13] Ibid.

[14] Ibid.

[15] Copher, p. 23.

[16] Diop, p. 51.

[17] M. C. Volney, *Travels Through Syria and Egypt,* Vol. I, trans. from the French. London: G. G. J. and J. Robinson, 1787, pp. 808.

[18] Hal Lindsey, *Combat Faith.* New York: Bantam Books, 1986, p. 110.

[19] Walker.

[20] Watchman Nee writes an excellent explanation of praise as a sacrifice. See "Assembling Together: Exercise thyself into godliness," 1 Timothy 4:7, Basic Lesson Series, Vol. 3, New York: Christian Fellowship Publishers, Inc., pp. 114, 115.

[21] Ibid.

[22] Walker. Dr. Walker humorously uses this well-known phrase in a clever application to hands lifted in praise to God.

[23] Ibid.

CHAPTER 10

[1] Charles B. Copher, *Black Biblical Studies, An Anthology of Charles B. Copher.* Chicago: Black Light Fellowship, 1993, p. 23.

[2] Daniel P. Mannix and Malcolm Cowley, *Black Cargoes: A History of the Atlantic Slave Trade 1518-1865.* New York: The Viking Press, 1962, p. xi.

[3] Ibid., p. 171.

[4] Ibid., p. 172.

[5] Ibid., p. 173.

[6] Ibid.

[7] Ibid., p. 174.

[8] Ibid.

[9] Ibid.

[10] Ibid.

[11] Ibid.

[12] Ibid., p. 177.

[13] Ibid.

[14] Ibid.

[15] Ibid.

[16] Ibid., pp. 179-185.

[17] Ibid., pp. 180-185.

[18] Ibid., p. 184.

[19] Ibid., p. 185.

[20] Ibid.

[21] Ibid.

[22] Thomas Carlyle, *The Nigger Question,* John Stuart Mill, *The Negro Question,* ed. Eugene R. August. New York: Appleton-Century-Crofts, 1971, vii.

[23] Ibid., p. vii.

[24] Ibid., p. viii.

[25] Ibid., p. vii.

[26] Charles B. Copher, "Biblical and Theological Issues on the Black Presence in the Bible," *Black Biblical Studies, An Anthology of Charles B. Copher*. Chicago: Black Light Fellowship, 1993, p. 23.

[27] Ibid., p. 23.

[28] *The New Merriam-Webster Dictionary*. Springfield, Mass.: Merriam-Webster, 1989, p. 47.

[29] Copher, p. 24. For a fuller discussion see also William Stanton, *The Leopard's Spots: Scientific Attitudes Toward Race In America 1815-59*. Chicago: The University of Chicago Press, 1960.

[30] For further review of Chancellor Williams' discussion on methods used to distort black history see *The Destruction of Black Civilization: Great Issues of a Race From 4500 B. C. to 2000 A. D.* Chicago: Third World Press, 1987, pp. 35-38.

[31] Ibid., p. 37.

[32] Dr. Yosef A. A. ben-Jochannan, *Black Man of the Nile*. Baltimore: Black Classic Press, 1989, p. 259.

[33] Ibid., p. 259.

[34] St. Clair Drake, *Black Folk Here and There: An Essay in History and Anthropology*. Los Angeles: Center for Afro-American Studies, University of California, 1987, vol. 1, 3rd printing, 1991, p. 137.

CHAPTER 11

[1] Gilbert Lewthwaite and Gregory Kane, "Witness to Slavery," *Baltimore Sun*. June 16, 1996, p. A1.

CHAPTER 12

[1] Elisabeth Kubler-Ross, *On Death and Dying*. New York: Simon & Schuster, 1970.

[2] Some of the concepts for understanding the grieving process have come from Bob Burns and Tom Whiteman, *The Fresh Start Workbook*. Nashville: Oliver Nelson, 1992, pp. 17-50.

CHAPTER 13

[1] Richard Bolles, *The Three Boxes of Life*. Berkeley, CA: Ten Speed Press, 1978, pp. 49-50.

CHAPTER 19

[1] Richard Bolles, *The Three Boxes of Life.* Berkeley, CA: Ten Speed Press, 1978, pp. 49-50.

[2] Ibid., pp. 163-165.

[3] Ibid., pp. 214-219.

[4] Nathan Aaseng, *The Locker Room Mirror.* New York: Walker and Company, 1993, p.11.

CHAPTER 20

[1] Carla Power and Allison Samuels, "Battling for Souls," *Newsweek.* October 30, 1995, p. 47.

CHAPTER 21

[1] Paul Zimmerman, *A Thinking Man's Guide to Pro Football.* New York: Simon Schuster, 1984, p. 12.

[2] C. Truman Davis, M.D., "The Crucifixion of Jesus," *Arizona Medicine.* Phoenix: March, 1965, p. 186.

[3] W. E. Vine, *An Expository Dictionary of New Testament Words.* Old Tappan, New Jersey: Fleming H. Revell, n.d., p. 156.

[4] Ibid., p. 83.

[5] George Perkins, ed. *The American Tradition in Literature.* New York: McGraw-Hill, 1990, pp. 1043-1044, (from *Narrative of the Life of Frederick Douglass,* 1845).

Selected Bibliography

ben-Jochannan, Yosef A. A. *Africa: Mother of Western Civilization.* Baltimore: Black Classic Press, 1988.

_____. *Black Man of the Nile and His Family.* Baltimore: Black Classic Press, 1989.

Bernal, Martin. *Black Athena: The Afroasiatic Roots of Classical Civilization,* Vol. I, *The Fabrication of Ancient Greece 1785-1985.* New Brunswick, New Jersey: Rutgers University Press, 1987.

_____. *Black Athena: The Afroasiatic Roots of Classical Civilization,* Vol. II, *The Archaeological and Documentary Evidence.* New Brunswick, New Jersey: Rutgers University Press, 1991.

Copher, Charles B. *Black Biblical Studies: Biblical and Theological Issues on the Black Presence in the Bible.* Chicago: Black Light Fellowship, 1993.

deGraft-Johnson, J. C. *African Glory: The Story of Vanished Negro Civilizations.* Baltimore: Black Classic Press, 1986.

_____. *Civilization or Barbarism: An Authentic Anthropology,* trans. Yaa-Lengi Meema Ngeuni, ed. Harold J. Salemson and Marjolijn de Jager. Brooklyn: Lawrence Hill Books, 1991.

Diop, Cheikh Anta. *The African Origin of Civilization: Myth or Reality,* ed. and tran. Mercer Cook. Westport, Conn.: Lawrence Hill & Company, 1974.

Evans, Anthony T. *Let's Get To Know Each Other: What White Christians Should Know About Black Christians.* Nashville: Thomas Nelson, 1995.

McCray, Walter Arthur. *The Black Presence in the Bible.* Chicago: Black Light Fellowship, 1990.

_____. *The Black Presence in the Bible and the Table of Nations.* Chicago: Black Light Fellowship, 1990.

McKissic, William Dwight, Sr. *Beyond Roots: In Search of Blacks in the Bible.* Wenonah, New Jersey: Renaissance Productions, 1990.

McKissic, William Dwight, Sr., and Anthony T. Evans. *Beyond Roots II:*

If Anybody Ask (sic.) You Who I Am. Wenonah, New Jersey: Renaissance Productions, 1994.

Perryman, Wayne. *Thought Provoking Bible Studies of The 90's.* Mercer Island, Washington: Consultants Confidential, 1993.

Snowden, Frank M., Jr. *Before Color Prejudice: The Ancient View of Blacks.* Cambridge, Mass.: Harvard University Press, 1983.

_____. *Blacks in Antiquity: Ethiopians in the Greco-Roman Experience.* Cambridge, Mass.: The Belknap Press of Harvard University Press, 1970.

Unger, Merrill F. *The New Unger's Bible Dictionary,* ed. R. K. Harrison. Chicago: Moody, 1988.

_____. *The New Unger's Bible Handbook,* rev. Gary N. Larson. Chicago: Moody, 1984.

Van Sertima, Ivan, ed. *Nile Valley Civilizations: Journal of African Civilizations.* New Brunswick, New Jersey: Rutgers University, 1986.

Van Sertima, Ivan. and Runoko Rashidi, eds. *African Presence in Early Asia.* New Brunswick, New Jersey: Transaction Books, 1988.

Van Sertima, Ivan, ed. *African Presence in Early Europe.* New Brunswick, New Jersey: Transaction Books, 1988.

Williams, Chancellor. *The Destruction of Black Civilization: Great Issues of A Race from 4500 B.C. to 2000 A.D.* Chicago: Third World Press, 1987.

Special Thanks

FROM DON

I am deeply grateful to my lovely wife, Brenda, for your sacrifice and commitment to me throughout this book project. The weekends and evenings spent with my writing and your typing are a labor of love that I'll always remember. May God richly bless you for your commitment to Jesus.

My sincere thanks to my friend and co-author, Joel Freeman, for your vision, encouragement and fearless commitment to advancing the kingdom of God. Without you this book would have never come into being.

FROM JOEL

I thank God every day for my precious wife, Shirley. Without your understanding of the time required to write and without your words of wisdom and encouragement—my part of this project would have never taken the shape that it has.

Don, you have demonstrated true friendship to me. Just about every day we have talked on the phone. During this time we have risked total honesty with and commitment to each other. Without this deep level of communication, *Return to Glory* would have been just another bright idea. My life has been changed because of your friendship and patience.

FROM BOTH DON AND JOEL

Dr. Clarence Walker, your exposition of Isaiah 18 provided us with our first insight into this very important passage. Hopefully, by God's grace, we have enhanced in some small way the message that God has brought through you. In addition, your counseling, advice and encouragement in ministering to African Americans has been very valuable.

Jeffrey Wright, your insights into the pain of the black experience in America has provided the framework from which the roadmap to wholeness has been built. You brilliantly communicated image, ideas, stories and concepts that fit well on paper.

Editor, Eugene Seals, you deserve special recognition for your editorial skills and patience in guiding us through the birth pains of bringing the manuscript to its final form.

Finally, to our publisher who persistently and with great wisdom keeps the focus on one primary goal—bringing glory to our Lord and Savior, Jesus Christ. May God richly bless Roland Hardy, his wife, Delores, and the Renaissance family as they strive to reach people of African descent with the good news of the Gospel.

The Authors

JOEL A. FREEMAN

Joel A. Freeman, author of three internationally acclaimed books, holds a Master of Science degree in counseling from Loyola College (Baltimore) and also holds a Ph. D. in the same discipline. He has served as chaplain for the NBA Washington Bullets/Wizards since 1979. As president of The Freeman Institute consulting firm, Dr. Freeman conducts team building/leadership/change management/cultural diversity initiatives for churches, corporations, U. S. government agencies, and the leaders of other nations. Joel, his wife, and family live in Maryland.

OTHER BOOKS BY JOEL A. FREEMAN

God Is Not Fair: Making Sense Out of Suffering

Living With Your Conscience Without Going Crazy

Kingdom Zoology: Dealing With the Wolves, Serpents and Swine in Your Life

DON B. GRIFFIN

Don B. Griffin holds a Bachelor of Arts degree in history from Lafayette College. A Bible teacher and preacher, Don conducts biblically based seminars on practical Christian living as well as pulpit ministry. He also is the top human resource executive for a $350 million corporation in the metro New York area. Don lives in Pennsylvania with his wife and son.

Other Books